DOING BUSINESS
IN THE
CZECH
REPUBLIC

THE AGE OF COMFORT IS HERE...

...ČSA Business Class

ALWAYS RELAXED AND IN GREAT FORM.

In ČSA Business Class,

even the most demanding travellers find their comfort. More space. Greater Comfort.
High-quality on-board services. Non-smoking flights.
Meals served on china. Personal assistance in world languages. And, on board our Airbus planes,
new flexible seats plus the Airshow programme
- information about the plane's location during the flight.
Relax!

AT HOME
IN THE SKIES

CBI

DOING BUSINESS IN THE CZECH REPUBLIC

CONSULTANT EDITOR: ADAM JOLLY

Contributing firms: McKenna & Co, Cerrex Ltd, VP International,
Creditanstalt, HSBC Group, Lubbock Fine, Seddons, PA Consulting,
Anglo-Czechoslovak Ventures, Research International, Gleeds, GJW,
CzechInvest, Prokop International, AWS, CEE Telecom Projects

KOGAN PAGE

Kogan Page Ltd
120 Pentonville Road
London N1 9JN
E-mail: kpinfo@kogan-page.co.uk

© Kogan Page 1997

British Library Cataloguing Data
A CIP record for this book is available from the British Library
ISBN 0 7494 1474X

Typeset by *JP Graphics Ltd*, London
Printed and bound in Great Britain by *Clays Ltd*, St Ives plc

Contents

Part 1 The Business Context

Part 2 Market Potential

Part 3 Business Development

Part 4 Building an Organisation

Part 5 Appendices

Foreword

The Czech Republic has established itself as a significant export market with a consistently strong set of macro-economic statistics. The round of elections which took place last year, have fully confirmed its democratic credentials and next year should see the start of its negotiations for full membership of the European Union. The Czech Republic is returning to where it should always have been – in the heart of Europe.

Nowhere in the region has privatisation been carried through so quickly and on such a large scale, although transferring the state's remaining holdings in energy, steel, transport and banking represents one of the major tasks for the new administration.

British companies have significant commitments in the market with investments to date of £400m. Bass has the largest presence, but Lucas, Tl and Avon Rubber, amongst others, have also bought into the Czech Republic's traditional industrial strengths. Tesco, Marks & Spencer and Vision Express are retailers with a place on the growing Czech high street.

Despite the Czech Republic's remarkable progress since the fall of Communism, problems still remain. Capital markets could be more transparent, there are some weaknesses in the banking sector and more could be done to restructure industrial capacity.

This book is designed to provide companies with practical advice on how best to identify and follow up opportunities in the Czech Republic. The CBI has been fortunate to draw on a wide range of experience and expertise: Creditanstalt, HSBC, McKenna, PA Consulting, Seddons, Lubbock Fine, Research International, Anglo-Czechoslovak Ventures, GJW, Gleeds, AWS and CzechInvest have all helped make possible, transactions, large and small, for international companies looking to grow in the market. Added to their commercial know-how, Cerrex, VP International, Prokop International and CEE Telecom Projects have provided a sector-by-sector breakdown of where the greatest areas of opportunity lie. Taken together, all these contributors have provided a rounded assessment of how best to develop in what has established itself as one of Eastern Europe's most interesting and progressive markets.

Adair Turner
Director General, Confederation of British Industry

The Contributors

Anglo-Czechoslovak Ventures Ltd has extensive experience gained over many years by assisting enterprises both in the UK and the Czech Republic with market entry and market development. The location of offices in London, Prague and Nitra in the Slovak Republic facilitates the support of clients' cross border trading activities. Michael Hermann, SF is chairman and founder of Anglo-Czechoslovak Ventures Ltd.

AWS Corporate Finance & Consultancy acts as an advisor to companies on most financing and accounting matters including raising trade and project finance, debt and equity and has particular expertise in Central and Eastern Europe and the Former Soviet Union. Kevin R Smith is a partner of AWS Corporate Finance & Consultancy.

CEE Telecom Projects is a marketing consultancy which assists with export, type approval, JVs and contacts with the regions Telcos. Ivan Sloboda MSc, CEng, MIEE, opened up the Czech and Slovak Republics for BT and PA, before moving to the DTI as a Telecom Export Promoter.

Cerrex Ltd is a London based research consultancy, specialising in export promotion and investment, trade relations policy, and helping companies access aid funds. Sectors in which they have been involved in the Czech Republic include electronics, consumer goods, glass, engineering, ceramics, energy and environment. Members of Cerrex Ltd act as advisors on energy and environment policy to the Czech Government. These articles were written by Michael Bird and Martin Doherty.

Creditanstalt has established the largest foreign-owned banking network in the region which includes a comprehensive range of commercial banking, investment banking, leasing and stock broking services. This expanding network presently covers Poland, Hungary, the Czech and Slovak Republics, Slovenia, Romania, Croatia and Bulgaria. Christian Kaltenegger previously worked within the Project Finance Division, he is now responsible for macro-economics research on the Czech Republic in Creditanstalt's Economics Department.

CzechInvest is the executive arm of government responsible for the attraction of foreign direct investment into the Czech Republic. Founded in 1992 CzechInvest has four departments, Marketing, Greenfield Projects, Joint Ventures and Regions with four representatives abroad in France, Germany, the UK and the USA. Aleš Ždimera works in the Regional Department of CzechInvest.

Eurotariff is the European arm of Worldtariff of San Francisco and is run from the offices of Cerrex Ltd in the UK. The firm are publishers of English versions of the customs tariffs for, among others, the major Central and Eastern European countries including the Czech Republic, Russia and the Ukraine. The company also undertakes research on customs related matters including origin and processing.

GJW is Europe's largest government relations consultancy with offices in London, Brussels, Prague, Budapest, Warsaw and a network of associates and agents throughout the remainder of Central and Eastern Europe. GJW enables firms to develop strategies against a sound understanding of present and future public policy, undertaking monitoring and research, offering strategic advice, lobbying, building contacts and carrying out political audits across a wide range of political issues. Andrew Ellis manages GJW's operations throughout Eastern Europe and Russia. Vladimir Feldman is a director at GJW.

Gleeds Prague office specialises in providing construction consultancy, cost and project management and property development advice to a wide range of Czech and international clients. Since 1991 Gleeds has acted as consultant on over US$100 million worth of completed construction in the Czech Republic. David Lawn is manager of Gleeds Prague office.

HSBC Investment Services Limited, Czech Republic, is a wholly owned subsidiary of HSBC Investment Bank plc. Jan Tauber, former advisor to the Minister of Finance in the first Czechoslovak post-Communist Government is a director of HSBC Investment Services Limited.

Lubbock Fine sro is the largest independent firm of chartered accountants operating in Central Europe. Its main office in the centre of Prague employs over 50 international Czech consultants, accountants, auditors and bookeepers who together offer a full range of services including business set-up, internal systems and audit, IT consulting and international reporting. They also specialise in local business consulting and tax planning and advice. Martin Levey is the managing partner of Lubbock Fine sro and a member of the International Tax Planning Association.

McKenna & Co is a major international law firm based in the City of London. It has offices in Almaty, Brussels, Budapest, Hong Kong, Moscow, Prague, Tashkent, Warsaw and Washington DC. McKenna & Co established itself in Central Europe in 1989 and has since expanded into Eastern Europe and Central Asia. The firm built up a wide range of commercial, governmental and legal contacts and provides its clients with legally sound, practical and commercial advice based on a thorough understanding of doing business in the region. Dr Irena Edwards is the Business Development Manager for Central Europe involved with strategic planning and market co-ordination of the firm's Prague, Warsaw and Budapest offices, and client development in the region. As of 1 May 1997 the firm will merge with the City law firm Cameron Markby Hewitt and will be known as Cameron McKenna.

PA Consulting Group, one of the world's leading management and technology consultancies, opened operations in the former Czechoslovakian Federal Republic in 1990. PA's focus is on the development and implementation of market facing business strategies and business processes, supported by strong IT, total quality, recruitment and human resource development capabilities. John Waugh has been running PA's consulting activities in Central Europe since early 1993, in the Prague office. He has in-depth experience of strategy formulation and implementation, business transformation, business process reengineering and human resource development in Czech, Slovak, Hungarian and Slovenian enterprises.

Prokop International Ltd is a specialist consultancy on FMCG in the former Eastern Europe, helping multinational companies with sales staff recruitment, training, merchandising and related activities. Michael Prokop is the managing director.

Research International World Service is a division of Research International – the world's largest custom market agency with offices in 54 countries spanning all the major continents. Mia Bartňová is a specialist in the newly emerged markets in Central and Eastern Europe.

Seddons is a multi-disciplinary legal practice serving international and local clients who wish to invest in the Czech Republic or Czech clients who wish to expand their business into Great Britain. The firm has been involved in the former Czechoslovakia since early 1990, initially acting for foreign clients wishing to set up subsidiaries/branches, to invest, to trade or conduct other activities in the Czech Republic. Jan Grozdanovič is a partner in Seddons with a special responsibility for the firm's Czech practice. Karin Pomaizlová is a junior associate at the Prague office, specialising in intellectual property law, conflict of laws and public international law.

VP International is one of the UK's leading Central European business services companies. As the UK's foremost supplier of English language business information from the region, VP International represents numerous highly regarded business directories, databases and newspapers produced in Poland, Hungary and the Czech Republic. At its office in Chester, VP International has one of the UK's most comprehensive collections of business information available for Central Europe; with an extensive range of up-to-date reports, press cuttings, exhibition catalogues and business publications. VP International has particular expertise in the automotive sector and currently works for several major UK automotive component companies throughout Poland and the Czech Republic. VP International also has offices in Prague and Warsaw.

Worldtariff are the parent company of Eurotariff and are based in San Francisco. They publish versions of the customs tariffs for all the major world trading nations including the Central and Eastern European countries.

THE CZECH REPUBLIC

Part One

The Business Context

Market Potential

Dr Irena Edwards, McKenna & Co

Czechoslovakia's 'velvet revolution' in November 1989 led to the establishment of many new parties: the most prominent being the Civic Forum, which went on to form the first post-Communist government. The first president was Vaclav Havel, the country's leading dissident playwright, the first Minister of Finance was Vaclav Klaus. This 'caretaker government' re-opened the country to the world and within a few months it had put in place the essential legal and institutional framework for a market economy.

The first 'real' democratic election took place in June 1992 and brought to government a right wing reformist coalition of the Civic Democratic Party and Civic Democratic Alliance led by Prime Minister Vaclav Klaus. The fast growing nationalist movement in Slovakia led by Vladimir Meciar resulted in January 1993 in the peaceful separation of Czechoslovakia into the Czech and Slovak Republics. The recent June 1996 election deprived Mr Klaus's coalition of a parliamentary majority and brought him to the negotiating table with the new force in Czech politics, the centre-left Czech Social Democratic Party under the leadership of Milos Zeman. Although there is no question of stopping the market oriented reforms, this development may slow the pace down as Mr Zeman's socially orientated policies often clash with Mr Klaus's hard 'Thatcherite' line.

Economic and investment climate

Under the leadership of Prime Minister Vaclav Klaus, the Czech Republic enjoyed a stable and relatively popular Government with clear, consistent market orientated policies. Statistically speaking the results are impressive: inflation has halved since 1993 to 9 per cent; unemployment is below 3 per cent; economic growth is around 5 per cent; the country has strong foreign currency reserves; the lowest foreign debt per capita and a very stable currency. These are by far the best economic statistics of any of the former East bloc countries. In 1989 the Czech Republic lost almost all of its traditional markets in the East, but by 1995 had refocused 60 per cent of its trade towards the West. It is no wonder that Moody's Investor Service raised its investment rating for the Czech Republic to Baal in September 1995. IBCA, the London based credit rating agency, assigned an A-rating in 1996- the first such rating given to a former COMECOM country.

In 1995 the Czech currency became almost fully convertible, thus removing one of the last remaining obstacles for the Republic to become the first post-Communist nation to join the OECD. The country is an Associate Member of the European Community with full membership anticipated around the year 2000.

With its position in the heart of Europe, a long industrial and distinguished cultural history, a well-educated and highly motivated workforce and 80 per cent of enterprises in private hands, it presents itself as a good trade and investment opportunity for British companies. Even the split of the country in 1993 seems to have benefitted the Czech Republic in terms of the industrial base and resources.

Regardless of these facts, inward UK trade and investment amounts to a mere 3 per cent; the Germans have 50 per cent of imports and 40 per cent of investment. The reasons are of course historical, geographical and practical. The proximity of Germany and Austria and their historical ties are significant, but so is the British obsession with its traditional markets to the exclusion of a territory which is only two hours away from London-Heathrow. The UK recession also played its role, as did the initial reluctance of British banks to finance business in the region.

The sceptics are quick to point out that there is still rather a lot to do and that the restructuring of the privatised economy has barely started: there is need for regulation and greater transparency of the Czech stock market; less domination of the market by local banks; better protection for minority shareholders; increase labour productivity; decrease the trade deficit - the list goes on.

The problems are well publicised and recognised. The Czech's themselves are very pragmatic and do not trust to miracles. They proved it amply in the June 1996 election by depriving Mr Klaus of his parliamentary majority. The problems will be sorted out. What counts and should give foreign investors confidence is not what is still to be done but what has been achieved in such a short time.

2

Economic Performance

Christian Kaltenegger, Creditanstalt

Background

Czechoslovakia first came into existence in 1918 as one of the major successors of the Austro-Hungarian monarchy and used to be one of the economically most advanced parts of the former empire, accounting for about 70 per cent of the industrial capacity of the territory. In 1939 the country was split into two, with the Czech part annexed by Germany and the Slovak part becoming a formally independent state. After World War II Czechoslovakia was reconstituted. Gaining the majority in the elections held in 1946, the Communists dominated a coalition goverment and finally took power in 1948. Since Czechoslovakia was a highly industrialised country that had not suffered too excessive war damages, the preconditions for Stalinist central planning seemed to be favourable. Nationalisation of industry and the collectivisation of agriculture was put forward quickly, creating an economy with very high levels of concentration and centralisation. The economy was geared towards the needs of industrialisation in the USSR and Eastern Europe, thus heavy industry was favoured and exports were directed mainly towards the East. The 1960s saw, though modest in the beginning, cultural, political and economic liberalisation, reaching a peak in the 'Prague Spring' in 1968. The freedom movement was suppressed by the invasion of Russian troops, but finally proved to be the seed for the 1989 'velvet revolution', which swept away Communist rule and paved the way for a solid political democracy.

The transition period

On 8 and 9 June 1990 the first free elections since 1946 were held, establishing the 'Civic Forum', the movement that initiated the velvet revolution, as the clear winner. Together with its Slovak counterpart, the 'Public Against Violence' movement, it formed a federal coalition government. The following two years saw a strong political differentiation within the Civic Forum, with the Civic Democratic Party, under Vaclav Klaus, becoming a clearly defined right-wing party and increasing alienation between the Czech and the Slovak parts of the country. The general elections in June 1992 confirmed these trends, with both Mr Klaus' party and Mr Meciar's left-wing 'Movement for a Democratic Slovakia' gaining equal support. This laid the foundation for the split between the two countries that came into effect on 1 January 1993.

The conditions for the transformation process of Czechoslovakia were quite favourable. Located in Central Europe and bordering Germany and Austria, the country is located close to important Western European markets. The macroeconomic structure was fairly advanced with engineering and electrical and metalworking accounting for 32 per cent of industrial production. Infrastructure was relatively favourable (eg in 1990, the CSFR had one telephone for every 3.6 inhabitants as opposed to one telephone for 5.5 inhabitants in Hungary). The education level was advanced, the average monthly wages low (1990: US$ 187). Inflation rates did not exceed 3-5 per cent, national debt was only 9 per cent and international debt 16 per cent of GDP in 1989.

However, the heritage was only favourable relative to other transforming economies; many problems remained to be resolved. Compared to western standards the structure of the economy was biased towards heavy industry with per capita steel production being 50 per cent higher than in Austria or Germany. The service sector and new technologies were underdeveloped.

In 1989, at the end of the centrally planned economy, 90 per cent of GDP was produced in the state sector and the average size of the firms in the productive sector was 4038 employees, which was extremely large compared to Austria (146 employees), Sweden (141) or Italy (79).

When the new post-Communist government came to power in 1989, it launched a very ambitious stabilisation programme with the help of the IMF. The initial transformation period between 1989 and 1991 was marked by the introduction of the following measures:

- The Czechoslovakian crown was devalued by as much as 100 per cent.

- On 1 January 1991 prices in most areas previously under state control were liberalised.

- Subsidies were cut by 36 per cent in 1991.

- The state monopoly of foreign trade was abolished in June 1990.

- A tight monetary policy kept growth of M2 (+26.9 per cent in 1991) well below inflation rate (+61.1 per cent). The authorities also achieved a large measure of fiscal contraction in 1991, as the general government deficit was reduced from 6.6 per cent of GDP in 1990 to nil in 1991.

• State-owned assets were privatised rapidly in the so-called 'small' privatisation, which encompassed restaurants, services and other local businesses and began in late January 1991. By the end of the year, as many as 25 000 enterprises were privatised.

• Large enterprises were supposed to be privatised under the 'large-scale privatisation law', which passed parliament in February 1991. However, it took more than a year, from 18 May to 9 June 1992, until the shares of the enterprises to be privatised were offered to the voucher-holders.

However, it was not until 1994, after four years of recession, with an overall decline in GDP of 20.7 per cent, that the adjustment-induced recession was over. This was caused on the one hand by supply factors since the quality of the existing fixed capital and labour could not immediately match the needs of a market economy. On the other hand, it was aggravated by lack of demand caused by a sharp decrease in real wages (nominal wages increased by only 16.5 per cent compared to the inflation rate of 61.1 per cent), high interest rates and monetary and fiscal austerity.

Recent economic development

Today, there are many good reasons why the Czech Republic is considered to be the success story of economic transition in Central and Eastern Europe: it has shown robust growth since 1994 and can boast the lowest unemployment in the region, a balanced state budget, strong foreign investment and a stable currency. The privatisation process was among the quickest and most readily accepted by the population. The Czech Republic was the first of the countries in transition to become a member of the OECD, in late 1995, and prospects of being among the first to join the EU are good. Until the elections of 31 May and 1 June 1996, Mr Klaus headed a stable coalition government, supported by a majority in Parliament. However, in this election the governing Conservative coalition was denied confirmation by the voters. Winning only 99 out of 200 seats, it lost its absolute majority and now works as a minority government.

The Social Democrats were able to establish themselves as the principal opposition. No severe political instability is expected to arise from the present stalemate: all parties – with the exception of the

Communists and the Republicans – fundementally agree on all important issues concerning European policies and the free market system. However, the ongoing transition process is very likely to slow down: reforms in government-owned enterprises, the privatisation of banks and a further liberalisation of prices in the housing and energy sectors will hardly be backed up by the Social Democrats. Mr Klaus has followed a policy of non-intervention in economic matters, so a government with less elbow-room should not prevent further economic upswing.

One of the prevailing economic problems is that of persistent inflation. While the Czech Republic's inflation rate of about 9 per cent is the lowest in all transition countries (with the exception of Slovakia), it is high by OECD standards. Keen demand for investment and consumer goods, the ongoing price liberalisation and wage dynamics, in particular in the service sector, have produced a sustained inflationary pressure. Therefore, the Czech National Bank's (CNB) focus clearly shifted towards further reduction of inflation. The Bank repeatedly expresses concern about the high inflation rate and emphasised its determination to impose a more restrictive monetary policy.

A strong domestic economy and rather sluggish demand in the main export markets, as well as a stronger crown, now trading nearly 3 per cent above the central parity of the mark/dollar basket, leads to soaring trade deficits, a problem that is expected to phase out gradually towards the year 2000. What will have to be watched carefully is the structure of imports. Investment goods form an important basis for upgrading the quality of the stock of capital investment in the Czech Republic. The adverse impact of the high trade deficit is lessened by a surplus of services which bring in handsome revenues from the tourist trade. The resulting current account deficit will easily be covered by a capital account surplus brought about by strong foreign investment in the crown. In 1995, the inflow of foreign direct investment reached US$ 2.6 billion, the highest amount since 1990; the overall capital account posted a surplus of US$ 8.4 billion.

Whereas inflation is being seriously tackled by the CNB, and the current account deficit, very much a consequence of the upswing in the domestic economy, is manageable, there is reasonable doubt that the restructuring of the economy has progressed fast enough so far. This doubt is supported by the moderate gains in labour productivity registered since 1989 compared with other countries in transition. The problem is, of course, that despite privatisation taking place comparatively quickly, changes in corporate governance have been rather modest, and state influence has in fact remained quite significant. The leading investment funds are owned by the major Czech banks, whose major shareholder (average holding: 40 per cent) is the National Property Fund. Overall, the NPF owns 20 per cent of the privatised companies. On the other hand, this is the very reason why there should be interesting investment opportunities in the pipeline since there is ample room for improvement on the company level within a stable and sound macroeconomic environment.

Given the large investment needs of the economy, efficient financial markets are crucial to furthering the success of the Czech Republic. While reforms in the banking sector are still rather sluggish, with ownership and control issues not very clear in many cases, there are some improvements being seen in the capital markets.

With its highly developed economic and political culture, its favourable blend of a highly skilled labour force with comparatively low wages, right at the heart of Europe, bordering Germany and Austria, all the odds are in the favour of the Czech Republic. Growth is expected at a pace of about 5 per cent annually during the next few years; inflation should come down slowly to western European standards and the current account should improve by 1998, with the help of a weaker crown. The challenge ahead for the Czech Republic will be to understand and to speed up the process of a permanent move towards international highly competitive economic structures.

3

A Political Overview

Andrew Ellis, GJW Holdings Ltd and Vladimir Feldman, GJW Prague

The Czech Republic has acquired a reputation as the shining star of free market political change in Central Europe. Democratic elections took place in 1990, 1992 and 1996: the process of splitting with Slovakia was managed peacefully with relative ease. Privatisation, especially through the innovation of the voucher scheme, was trumpeted as an early big success, with the Czech experience now being used as a model by the World Bank; and the currency has maintained its value better than any in the region (and several within the European Union).

Is all as rosy as it seems?

The answer to this question lies above all with the man associated most intimately with the politics of the transition: the Prime Minister, Vaclav Klaus. Klaus, leader of the major party of government, the ODS (Civic Democratic Party), has built a reputation as a strongly 'Thatcherite' economic reformer. He is a forceful personality not known to brook argument. Yet even before the election, the 'Thatcherite' revolution had become in many ways as much window dressing as reality. The lack of controls on privatisation meant that control of much of Czech industry moved in practice into the hands of the banks, which are not sufficiently well organised to be able to restructure and develop the businesses they acquired. Some large parts of State assets, for example Transgas and the National Forestry Company, remain firmly in State hands and the number of bankruptcies remained low throughout, as Klaus the canny politician took decisions that certainly did not conform with the ideology.

The political institutions of the Czech republic have solidified and now have a clear and accepted form. Klaus's party has remained the largest in the Czech Parliament throughout. In coalition with the ODA (Civic Democratic Alliance, right-wing Liberals) and the KDU-CSL (Christian Democrats), it governed with an overall majority before the

1996 general election, and still forms the government with the same coalition – this time two seats short of the overall majority. The coalition before the election was usually firmly driven by Klaus and ODS: since the election the KDU-CSL in particular has realised its increased bargaining power, as shown by a significant decision for the restitution of some church land.

The major opposition party is the CSSD (Social Democrats) led by Milos Zeman, which gained significantly in the 1996 elections. The remaining seats are held by the Communists and the ultra-right Republicans. Since the election, the Social Democrats have been waging a strong media onslaught against the government. Although this has been to some extent populist, it is clearly striking a chord with the public – signs of tiredness with the Klaus era are now emerging, later and as yet less strongly than in Poland or Hungary, but present nonetheless. The Social Democrats have sensed the possibility of early elections, at which they might make further gains. In the meantime, the Klaus government has had to start to learn the art of negotiation with opponents and building a majority.

The Social Democrat programme includes the freezing of state interests in strategic banks and companies, and a stronger government role in planning the economy. The party is, however, very definitely not a reborn Communist party. Its coming to power should not be regarded as a threat in itself to business or to the stability of the country – any more than the left wing victories in Poland and Hungary have undermined the long-term stability and direction achieved by those countries. A change of government at the next election should be regarded as a normal swing of the pendulum.

The future

Despite the political uncertainty, the Czech Republic has nonetheless maintained its leading position as an attraction for western investment, and a continued growth rate of 5 per cent up to the turn of the century is forecast. But confidence in the banking sector has fallen as a result of high profile bank failures, and the foreign trade deficit has soared, leading the opposition to accuse the government of doing nothing to help Czech companies. If the trade deficit reaches 7 per cent of GNP next year, the value of the crown will be in doubt – even though the country's overall foreign currency reserves represent four-fifths of the national budget, which the Ministry of Finance states can remain balanced. It is a long way from the days when Klaus was able to point to the crown as meeting the convergence criteria of the European exchange rate mechanism (ERM), and even talk of revaluation.

Prime Minister Klaus attributes the foreign trade deficit to high spending at home and inward investments, and points to the fact that the value of Czech exports has only decreased in the agricultural sector. Nonetheless, after the initial speed of the transition, a sense of drift has replaced the earlier momentum. It is not clear where the government wants to go next, even if it were in overall control. Almost shades of Harold Wilson.

The question for business trading or investing in the Czech Republic is whether a government that is beginning to run out of steam causes a serious problem. The indications are that as long as one is careful, and watches the particular issues that might be of interest to an incoming government or coalition of a more socialist tinge, the market and the climate for successful activity will remain.

4

Social and Consumer Trends

Mia Bartoňová, Research International World Service

Overview

Czech consumers continue to adapt and evolve in the new market economy environment. Brands have begun to acquire images, consumers have more knowledge about and can differentiate between products based on brand image, not just based on brand awareness – ie the names of products.

Local brands are experiencing a renaissance, particularly in the food and personal products sectors. The rise in the popularity of local brands is due partly to the lower cost (compared to western brands), partly to the improved product offering of the local brands (increased quality, better packaging and promotion) and partly to increased nationalism (many consumers prefer to buy a local brand if the quality is acceptable).

Shopping behaviour has changed in the last two years: most consumers no longer shop daily (or twice a day), but shop for fresh items several times a week and tend to do 'bigger' shopping once a fortnight or once a month. Many new supermarkets have been built in the last two years and many more are under construction. Already 15 per cent of the total food turnover in Prague is sold through western-style self service supermarkets. This proportion is almost certain to increase.

In 1995 over one-third of the Czech adult population were saving regularly; about a third of the GDP was placed in savings in the last year.

The salaries of employed staff were beginning to keep up with the rises in the cost of living. However energy prices are set to rise substantially over the next few months, thus creating inflationary pressures and placing further demands on the already limited disposable income.

Economic background

According to the Czech Ministry of Finance (macroeconomic indicators for 1996/97), in summer 1996, the outlook for the Czech economy was good. It was expected to grow faster than in 1995, the GDP growth was envisaged to be around 5.5 per cent (5.2 per cent in 1995), inflation was to be lower than last year (at 9 per cent) with unemployment at around 3.5 per cent.

The population was optimistic about the outlook for the next year (1996/97), with more expecting an improvement than a decline. However, after the elections in summer 1996, when the political canvas shifted to the left, there was a reversal of views, with a greater proportion of the population expecting the economic situation to worsen.

Q. Do you think that the overall economic situation will be better, worse or the same in one year from now?

	January 1996 %	August 1996 %
Better	32	14
Worse	24	29
Same	37	44
Don't know/Not sure	7	13

Source: Opinion Window – RI

After the election fewer people believed that the new government was taking the country in the right direction.

Q. Would you say that the political development of the Czech Republic is going in the right or wrong direction?

	January 1996 %	August 1996 %
Right direction	51	32
Wrong direction	31	34
Don't know/Not sure	18	35

Source: Opinion Window – RI

Demographics

The demographic profile of the 10.4 million Czechs has remained stable in the last few years and is similar to Western European nations.

Table 4.1 Demographic profile of the Czech population (1991)

	%
Male	48
Female	52
AGE	
up to 14 years	20
15–24 years	15
25–39 years	21
40–54 years	22
55+ years	22

Source: Statistical Yearbook of Czech Republic 1994

Since this last census the average size of a household has been around 2.5 individuals.

Cost of living

Between 1989 and 1994 the cost of living for households with employees has increased by two and half times. The increase in services (this category covers rent, energy and municipal energy) was the highest.

Table 4.2 Cost of living increases 1989–1994

Year	Total	Food	Non–Food	Services
1989	100	100	100	100
1990	109.9	113.7	110.4	106.1
1991	168.1	168.5	181.4	148.0
1992	187.3	184.3	197.3	184.0
1993	226.2	215.5	236.1	236.5
1994	249.8	237.0	257.3	275.8

Source: Statistical Yearbook of Czech Republic 1995

Between 1991 and 1993 (when relevant government official data was available) the increase in incomes had not kept pace with the rises in cost of living, resulting in the population having to draw on their savings and having to adjust their consumption.

Table 4.3 Income v. cost of living

	1992/1991	1993/1992
Income	109.1	126.6
Cost of living	111.4	120.8

Source: Statistical Yearbook of Czech Republic 1994

Household expenditure

Food continued to be the largest item of expenditure for all households. In 1995 one-third to one-half of household disposable income was spent on food. Rent and municipal services (electricity, gas, etc) accounted for about 20 per cent of disposable income. The cost of energy has risen in the winter of 1996; some estimates put the increases at up to 30 per cent.

The proportion of the population which intends to purchase a new motorcar and/or a property has remained the same since 1992, with 12 per cent intending to buy a new motorcar in the next two years while 3 per cent intend to purchase a property (*Source:* Gfk Prague).

Savings

The rates of savings are increasing again after three years of decline. When the Wall fell, savings initially remained high due to people's reluctance to spend when they were uncertain of what the future might bring. As the markets opened, the Czechs, together with the other Eastern Europeans, began spending on newly available western goods, and savings slumped. In 1995, inflation had been falling and real wages rising, thus the Czechs have again started to save.

Czech private savers saved the equivalent of about 36 per cent of the country's gross domestic product in the last year. The majority of the savings originated from a minority of the population (individuals with above average saleries). Over one-third of all households were planning to save some money, but were not sure whether they would manage it, whilst nearly a half did not manage to save anything, living from one payday to the next. The latter group was unable to save money, not because of high/extravagant spending but because their income was too low to enable them to save (*source:* Gfk Prague).

Table **4.4** Czech private savings 1991–1995, as % of GDP

Year	Private Savings as % of GDP
1991	30
1992	25
1993	28
1994	30
1995	36

Source: J.P Morgan, London

Shopping

The change in shopping patterns in the Czech Republic has been mainly due to the change in the infrastructure of the retail food business and, to a lesser extent, the changes in working habits/patterns.

In the last two years several self-service western-style supermarkets have been established in most large towns in the Czech Republic. Although the choice of supermarkets/food outlets is less extensive than in Western European countries' many western retailers (for example Delvita, Meinl, Pronto and Tesco) now have many outlets across the country. In Prague, where the choice of food outlets is greatest, about 15 per cent of food purchases are made in branded supermarkets.

Supermarkets have attracted the more affluent, younger (20–25 years age group) shoppers, mainly women and those with a better education. In many cases these women work, thus are attracted by the 'one-stop shop' convenience of the supermarkets.

Pensioners and the less well off continue to visit several local food outlets daily in order to compare prices.

Branding

During the first two to three years after the fall of the Wall, Czech consumers were exposed to a large number of western brands. Many had heard a variety of brand names (eg Sony, Mercedes, Levis, Suchard, Lipton's) but most only knew *of* them, rather than being familiar with such goods.

The learning curve undertaken by most consumers in the early nineties was steep. Many learned, from experience, that *'not all from the West is the best'*. Several large multinationals supplied non-Western European product formulations in the Czech Republic and other

Central European countries. Czech consumers not only learned that western products differed in quality – initially many believed that *all* western products were superior to local brands – but also, that one brand could have varyable quality depending on whether it was purchased/manufactured in a western country or in Central Europe, Middle East or Africa.

Local brands, with few exceptions previously unknown, began emerging, some created in conjunction with western manufacturers' others by the newly privatised Czech companies which revitalised many old products by new packaging and advertising together with improvement in quality. The emergence of higher quality (compared to pre-1990) local brands supported by advertising led many consumers to the realisation that some high quality local brands were as good, if not better, than some western brands.

Based on market research on branding carried out in the Czech Republic by the major research companies (Aisa, Gfk, Research International, etc) several new major trends were identified in consumer behaviour during 1995:

- **Growth in brand image:** most consumers now not only know/ have heard of brand names, but also have an image/idea of the properties/claimed benefits of the product.

- **Renaissance of local brands:** particularly in the food and personal products areas.

- **Local food products tend to be better suited:** to consumer tastes. Local brands also have an advantage in terms of price, most tending to be cheaper than their western counterparts.

- **Personal care products:** here the international brands probably have an advantage over domestic brands, but the exorbitant price difference (international products cost three to four times as much as the local ones) has led to faster growth of domestic brands. There is some evidence that the leading multinational brands of cleaning agents and detergents are less effected than the lesser-known brands from middle-sized or small producers.

- **Beverages:** the big international brands (eg Tchibo, Jacob's, Coca Cola and Lipton's) appear to be having a negative affect upon loyalty to domestic brands.

- **Rise of patriotism:** although the increased usage of local brands appears to be mainly due to their competitive/cheaper price, together with the improved quality of most of the local brands, a less marked, but nevertheless important element of the decision making process has been emerging in the last year or so. Some consumers express a preference for local brands on the basis of patriotism. They cite the wish to support local manufacturers particularly as many have significantly improved the quality of the local brands. This increase in national pride is present to a greater or lesser extent in all the Central European countries, although it is most marked in Poland.

Ownership of communication/IT

The telecommunication infrastructure has improved, particularly in the large towns in 1995. Telephone penetration and ownership of personal computers in the Czech Republic are amongst the highest in Eastern Europe, though still far behind Germany and the US. Digital networks are being overlaid over the outdated analogue system and about half a million consumers who have been waiting for a telephone line for the last 10 years have been told that their wait should be over by early 1997.

Table 4.5 Comparison of telecommunication infrastructure

Number per 1,000 people	Czech Republic	Hungary	Poland	Germany	USA
Telephone lines	359	208	197	501	598
Cellular subscribers	4.6	13.5	1.1	30.3	92.7
Computers	48	49	28	174	360
Connections to Internet	1.66	1.09	0.67	5.85	21.82

Source: World Connectiveness Yearbook 1996

5

Trade Relations with the European Union

Cerrex Ltd

Since 1990 trade relations between the Czech Republic and the European Union have become progressively closer with rapidly increasing reciprocal trade. The EU has opened its market to exports from the Czech republic, mainly through the abolition or suspension of most quantitative restrictions (QRs), granting preferential tariff access, and trade and economic cooperation agreements complemented by an aid programme (Phare).

At the end of 1994, the EU agreed a pre-accession strategy for those Central European, including the Czech Republic, and other countries wishing to join. *The EU – Czech Association Agreement* provides for close bilateral cooperation between the two over a period of 5–10 years, including:

1. Trade. The gradual establishment of a free trade area. Imports of Czech industrial goods enter the EU duty free, although transitional tariff arrangements for textiles expire at the end of 1997. The speed of concessions varies according to the product concerned. EU tariffs on about 50 per cent of goods were abolished immediately the agreement came into force on 1 January 1993. Agricultural and processed foods are dealt with separately over a longer time scale. All quantitative restrictions on industrial goods were phased out immediately, or are timed to expire by the end of 1996. The agreement includes the establishment of a more favourable origin, trade policy and anti-dumping trade framework.

2. The gradual alignment of Czech law with EU internal market legislation. The extent of the progress towards adoption of Union legislation (the *acquis communautaire*) is be one of the factors which the Commission considers in drafting its opinion as to whether the country is ready for membership.

3. Guarantees covering freedom to transfer funds, repatriation of

properties and certain legal rights such as free movement of workers and freedom to establish services, and a framework for economic cooperation covering promotion and protection of investment, adoption of standards, scientific and technical cooperation, training and education, regional development, small and medium enterprises, statistical cooperation, combined action against money laundering and drugs, the environment, transport, telecommunications.

4. Closer cooperation and resolution of any potential areas of conflict through a series of regular Councils between ministers responsible for the internal market, economics and finance. Czech officials are also present at EU meetings covering trade related matters including economic integration. This includes services, establishment and operation of enterprises, competition, public procurement, economic cooperation, approximation of laws, cultural and financial cooperation and agriculture and fisheries.

5. Aid funding. An enlarged technical assistance and financial support programme is planned under the Phare programme, increasingly aimed at pre-accession activity, as well as cultural cooperation.

The concept of the structured dialogue

Running in tandem with the arrangements under the Association Agreements is the 'structured dialogue'. This provides a forum for the EU and applicant states as a group to meet the institutions of the Union on a multilateral basis, and to consider issues of common interest such as energy, environment, agricultural policy – (where the major issue is consideration of the reports by the Commission on agricultural policy in the light of enlargement) – and to a lesser extent education, and practical cooperation in areas of Common Foreign and Security Policy and Justice and Home Affairs.

Reorganisation of Phare

Phare is the main channel for European financial assistance to the Czech Republic. When first established, it was designed to support the process of economic restructuring and the development of the market economy. The scheme for 1995–99 was modified so that multi-annual sectoral programmes (replacing annual schemes) were introduced and greater emphasis put into areas of medium term financial adjustment, co-financing with financial institutions such as EBRD, and supporting the pre-accession strategy.

Phare funds are now directed mainly into areas necessary to support the policy reforms essential for membership. Czech priorities are public administration reform such as customs and statistics, industrial property, competition and standards administration, cross-border cooperation with the EU in transport, energy and environment, small and medium enterprise (SME) development, regional development and the promotion of foreign investment – all areas which present opportunities for UK business. Funding in areas where Phare has traditionally been active such as energy, environment, human resource development, social sector, banking and finance, and agriculture, continues.

Promoting cooperation among Central European countries

Through the Europe Agreements and the Phare programme, the European Union has taken a number of initiatives to promote economic cooperation among the Central European countries and improve the investment climate including the Central European Free Trade Agreement (CEFTA), leading to free trade among the Czech Republic, Slovakia, Hungary and Poland and potentially others, and amendment to the EU origin rules to encourage 'pan-European cumulation'.

'Internal Market White Paper' (COM 95 (163))

When it accedes, the Czech Republic will have to implement all Community legislation and practices referred to in the *acquis communautaire*.

The White Paper was published to help bring the associated countries into line with EU internal market legislation. It describes the administrative and organisational structures in each sector if the legislation is to be effectively enforced and sets out a logical sequence for adopting internal market measures. The Czech Republic has shown considerable speed in adopting EU legislation, and in many sectors Czech legislation is now in line with that applicable to the 15. Any problems faced by UK exporters because Czech law does not conform to EU law can be raised in the Association Committee which implements the Europe Agreement.

Possible time table for entry

Negotiations with the Czech Republic and other CEEC/Baltic states and Slovenia are due to start immediately after the signature of the conclusion of the Inter-Governmental Conference (IGC) and once the

Council has given a mandate (ie at the beginning of 1998) if, as is expected, the Inter-Governmental Conference finishes in July 1997. By the end of IGC, the Commission will have prepared an 'avis' (opinion) on the application from the Czech Republic and negotiations will take place on the basis of this. No date has been fixed by which the negotiations must be concluded or by which new members must join. Many prominent Czechs have expressed the hope that entry would take place during the early part of the next decade, and Mr Klaus has said that he would like the Czech Republic to join without significant derogation from the 'acquis.'

Some major issues within the negotiations

It seems likely that the Czech Republic would be ready for membership before, for example, Poland or Bulgaria, where agricultural reform could be a greater problem and where there are greater administrative or institutional difficulties. The Czech Republic has a number of advantages:

- The government is politically sound and popular.

- The Czechs have taken steps, including the purchase of USA and EU military equipment, to come nearer to NATO, have strongly supported the EU position in the Gulf and there appears to be little objection from the Russians to its eventual membership.

- The Czech Republic was the first Central European state to join the Paris based OECD, the first to obtain an A rating from Standard and Poors and to make its currency freely convertible.

- It is closer to meeting the Maastricht criteria than any of its neighbours (and many of the present EU members).

- Czech macro-economic policy is sound. Inflation is projected to be under 5 per cent by 1998 and 3 per cent by the end of the century, and in many respects the Czech Republic is poised to overtake several EU countries within the decade.

Accession will, nonetheless, face a number of problems. Its transition to membership will probably be more comparable with the memberships of Spain and Portugal – a seven-year transition with slower steps in sensitive areas – than with accession of Austria, Finland and Sweden. A revision of the Common Agricultural Policy (CAP) could remove one of the main difficulties (although agriculture is less of a difficulty for the Czech Republic than for other Eastern European countries). A second major problem will be access to regional funds – under existing EU policy any region with a per capita GDP (Gross

Domestic Product) of less than 75 per cent of the EU average is eligible for assistance. Not only, therefore, would the Czech Republic qualify at present but at a GDP per capita of $4800, the Czech Republic would require 8–10 years at a growth of over 10 per cent before it could achieve the EU average. Until then, there will be concern about the extent of immigration into the EU, and the effects of adopting a policy of free movement of labour. There will also be problems over the free movement of financial services, competition policy, energy, transport, meeting environmental and social policy and consumer protection standards, and expatriation of land and property.

The indications are that although some of the Republic's major companies are competitive, many of the middle range might not survive an 'open market' and the country would have to revise its policy of holding down unemployment by continuing to give assistance to uncompetitive factories. A fully open market would also 'suck' raw materials away from the Czech Republic into the EU – the recent introduction of a licensing system to reduce corn exports and problems caused to the leather-goods industry because of the attraction of the raw leather producers to the higher EU prices are examples of this.

6

Privatisation

Jan Tauber, HSBC Investment Services sro

Before the collapse of the centrally planned economic system in 1989 Czechoslovakia was one of the countries with the highest percentage of state owned assets (95 per cent). The transfer of state property to private hands has been achieved through a combination of direct disposals of state-owned enterprises to domestic and foreign buyers and through the innovative application of the voucher privatisation scheme.

Since 1989 the subsequent Czechoslovak and later Czech governments have been emphasising that the pace of privatisation represents one of the most important criteria of the successful transformation from planned economy to the market system. Therefore, the speed of the transfer of property titles must be given priority over the legal and institutional aspects of this profound change of property relations.

Voucher privatisation

Two waves of voucher privatisation were decided upon, transferring shares of approximately 60 per cent of state-owned companies to either individuals or investment funds in several rounds of bidding process. Every citizen over the age of 18 had a right to buy a book of vouchers for CZK 1000 which gave him/her a chance to bid directly for shares in companies which were being privatised.

In practice, however, the overwhelming majority of people was not familiar with the corporate landscape and financial instruments and institutions. Therefore, instead of investing their investment points directly to offered companies they entrusted their voucher books (each voucher book contained 1000 investment points) to investment privatisation funds in which they became shareholders. Thus, through the collection of investment points from the general public, these funds have concentrated a substantial amount of assets and holdings in the privatised companies and acquired a considerable economic power. However, the investment privatisation funds have been often linked to the large and still partially state-owned banks and these banks have been simultaneously lenders to the companies where their funds have controlling stakes. Due to the missing legislation (insufficient 'Chinese Walls' between the funds and their parent banks) the funds are to a certain extent 'originators and guarantors' of the commercial banking business for their parent banks in the companies where they have holdings. This situation naturally complicates a sound development of domestic capital market and it is not conducive to the much-needed growth of its liquidity.

The voucher privatisation scheme thus brought about a change merely in the ownership structure of privatised companies but did not generate any new capital investment. The Prague Stock Exchange and the Czech capital market in general are still perceived by the local investing public more as a mere mechanism for obtaining control of companies which were brought to the Exchange by the voucher privatisation rather than looked at as a vehicle for raising capital for further growth and development of listed firms. The lack of capital of the recently privatised companies has therefore led to a situation in which investment privatisation funds gradually begin to realise that they are not able to manage efficiently companies which they control and thus enhance the value for their shareholders. They themselves, and often in cooperation with their parent banks, may initiate a search for strategic investors which should bring to these companies new capital with necessary know-how and modern technology.

Private buyers

Some of the state-owned enterprises were sold directly to previously identified foreign or domestic investors. Companies acquired by domestic buyers were often privatised through management buyouts (MBO) and because these transactions were funded almost exclusively by bank loans it was only natural that this method of privatisation led to a great number of firms being highly indebted and heavily under-capitalised. These firms are also currently forced to seek equity financing from both strategic and financial investors in order to strengthen their capital base. Some of the medium-sized and small companies, mainly from the manufacturing sector, with relatively high level of indebtedness, thus represent a natural target for potential overseas investors as well.

The remaining shares in companies that have not been fully privatised or shares in the strategic state-owned enterprises have been transferred to the National Property Fund (NPF), a state agency charged with legal and administrative issues of the transfer of state-owned assets to private buyers. The government thus maintains controlling interests in about 50 companies of strategic importance, such as the main electricity generator and distributor utility ČEZ, the

Czech railways, major steel and heavy engineering producers Nová Hut and Vitkovice, major gas supplier Transgas as well as all regional electricity and gas distributors. Through the NPF the government also holds significant stakes in the four largest Czech commercial banks: Komerčni Banka, Česká Spořitelna (Czech Savings Bank), Investični a Poštovni Banka (Investment and Postal Bank) and Československá Obchodni Banka (Czechoslovak Trade Bank).

The decision regarding the privatisation of these companies, as well as its timing and methods, are currently a subject of political discussions. Main issues raised in the debate deal with the problems which strategic companies should remain in the realm of public domain and in which form and to what extent, which companies should be privatised and offered through the public offerings or through trade sales to strategic investors, etc. The outcome of this debate very much depends on the balance of political forces in the country. There is, however, a general consensus prevailing across the political spectrum that the country needs foreign investment and that this investment should be supported.

Advantages and potential problems for investors

Advantages for international companies seeking investment opportunities in the Czech Republic could be summarised by the following:

● long and well-established industrial tradition, mainly in manufacturing industries;

● highly skilled and still relatively cheap labour force;

● stable macroeconomic environment in comparison with other former COMECON countries;

● no restrictions on foreign ownership and participation in joint ventures and Czech legal entities with the exception of the banking and defence sectors.

Main problems or potential risks for strategic investors may lie in the following areas:

● less transparent and still rather volatile legal and institutional environment;

● lack of expertise and experience in financial and marketing matters by the local senior management;

● insufficient depth and lack of liquidity of the domestic capital market.

7

Banking

VP International

One of the main troubles with the Czech banking sector is that the State simply doesn't want to give up control. After five years of so-called reform and consolidation, the country is left with quasi-privatisation which fails to satisfy the long-term requirements of a competitive, market-led economy necessitating radical restructuring. Government control is, however, just one of the many trials and tribulations afflicting the Czech banking sector.

Leading up to the present situation there has been a period of extreme instability during which many small banks opened and issued credits without any formal risk management. The result has been that, since 1994, eleven banks have failed, including the Plzen-based *Kreditni banka*, with losses of CZK 12 billion. In 1991 the government set up the *Konsolidacni banka* specifically to take over the credits arising from state-controlled companies. At the time of writing, *Agrobanka*, the country's largest wholly private financial institution, is also suffering related problems and its CZK 40 billion deposits are having to be guaranteed by the Czech National Bank (CNB). With this backing from the CNB, Frankfurt-based CommerzBank was happy to agree a credit facility of CZK 2 billion to the troubled bank.

Simultaneously, the CNB has launched a voluntary 'prevention programme' whereby it will take over bad loans to small private banks. Under the scheme banks are allowed to write off assets representing up to 110 per cent of their outstanding share capital. Any losses will be met by either one of two state financial institutions – the *National Property Fund* or *Konsolidacni banka*. It seems the government is anxious to maintain stability in the banking sector at almost any cost to the taxpayer.

State control

The state has a controlling share in the country's four largest banks:

	Government Voting Shares (%)
Komercni banka	54
Ceska Sporitelna	45
Investicni a Postovni banka (IPB)	31.5
Ceskoslovenska Obchodni (CSOB)	89

Together these four banks control approximately 70 per cent of the domestic banking market and exert enormous influence over the economy through their investment funds. The *CSOB* and *Sporitelna* together control 24 per cent of the loan market and 41 per cent of the investment market. At year end 1995 their combined capital totalled $1.23 billion.

In spite of a two year period of consolidation and reform, during which stringent new criteria were drawn up for the issuing of licences, it is generally believed that the big four banks may not have made adequate bad debt provisions and that they are still lending for political rather than for wholly commercial reasons. Despite a tightening up of auditing procedures, the full extent of their risk exposure is not yet fully known.

Nevertheless Czech banking is considered to be among the most advanced and safest in the region and has been given an 'A' long-term rating by Standard and Poors. *Zivnostenska banka*, for example, is the country's sixth largest bank and first in terms of dividend yield per share price. On anticipated 1996 profits of CZK 435–440 million it is expected to pay a gross dividend of CZK 170. Just 1 per cent of its total loan portfolio is believed to comprise risky credit. The bank is majority owned by BHF Bank AG (47 per cent) and IFC (10 per cent).

Privatisation

In order to attract much needed capital to fund development the Czech government have introduced a 'voucher' system of privatisation, which enables private investors to purchase Global Depository Receipts (GDRs). These are like ordinary shares, tradable on international bourses, but which offer no voting rights, thus protecting management control. However, in view of the overall profitability of the leading Czech banks, GDRs have proved quite popular. So while the sale of GDRs seemingly distances the state from individual privatisations, the resultant scattered private ownership of the banking sector means, in effect, the state maintains control over Czech industry, inhibiting its

competitiveness and even posing a threat to the stability of the entire industrial market. Other suggested methods of introducing outside capital are through negotiated deals with selected buyers or tenders/auctions.

While the government is anxious to accelerate the rate of privatisation of the major banks, it retains a blocking minority stake of 34 per cent enabling it to veto key decisions where necessary. Towards the end of 1996 the CNB produced a report recommending the merger of *Ceska Sporitelna* and *CSOB* to create the nation's largest semi-private bank with assets of over $20 billion, compared to $14.8 billion for *Komercni banka* and $7.9 billion for IPB.

The result of such a merger would postpone privatisation by three to five years to allow the industry to adjust to such large-scale change. However, the plan has met opposition on the basis that the resultant corporation would have too strong a hold on the domestic banking market and that it would be an operational and logistical nightmare.

The CSB is encouraging Czech banks to develop along the German (stakeholder) lines rather than the Anglo-Saxon model. This is seen as a strategic error as the former system is being re-examined by the Germans themselves, who are acknowledging the need for Anglo-Saxon style specialisation of financial services in order to develop their share of the corporate finance market.

Opportunity

Foreign banks can buy into existing Czech banks through GDRs, thus
avoiding the process of obtaining lengthy CNB approval. For example,
in May 1996 Komercni banka launched its second tranche of GDRs,
raising $55 million, equivalent to 10 per cent of the bank's capital.
However, such a route must be accompanied by maximum disclosure
and exit possibility assurances – two things for which the Czech market
is not noted.

A strategic investor could make a direct purchase from the state for
which it might have to pay an estimated 15 per cent premium. However,
such a negotiated deal offers the benefits of gaining maximum influence
over the targeted bank, exclusivity and a better chance to tailor a more
precise deal structure to suit its own requirements. From the Czech
point of view the tender/auction route would attract higher prices and
would be quicker but may be less attractive to foreign investors.

Česká pojišt'ovna a.s. – a leading insurance company

Česká pojišt'ovna a.s., the leading insurance company in the Czech Republic, has a very long and interesting history. The company is generally considered to be the direct successor of the first insurance company on the territory of today's Czech Republic, which was founded in 1827 (The First Bohemian Mutual Insurance Company).

Over the years Česká pojišt'ovna has grown into a truly general insurance company, offering the widest range of products and services to clients. At the same time, thanks to extensive reinsurance contacts with most of the leading insurance and reinsurance companies in all of the important world markets, it has gained an excellent international reputation.

Česká pojišt'ovna is a member of the International Union of Aviation Insurers, International Union of Marine Insurance, International Credit Insurance Association, Association of Hail Insurers and the Council of Bureaux. For many years it has also provided essential services to the international insurance community as Lloyds Agent for the territory of former Czechoslovakia and now the territory of the Czech Republic.

The modern history of Česká pojišt'ovna started to be written during 1991 after the new insurance act came into force. The essential change in the law created space for further development of the insurance industry in the Czech Republic within the new economic conditions and gave rise to a truly competitive environment following the abolition of the former state insurance company's monopoly. From the very beginning Česká pojišt'ovna has played a major role in this challenging development and also became an active member of the Czech Insurance Association.

The long-term strategy of Česká pojišt'ovna is to achieve the level of insurance service quality which is usual in the countries of the European Union, and to strengthen the leading position of the company on the Czech insurance market.

During the years after the termination of the state insurance company's monopoly this meant first of all widening Česká pojišt'ovna orientation on comprehensive satisfaction of all client needs and also continuation of the process of renewing the economic balance of those types of insurance which still suffered from tariff insufficiency left over from the past. The year 1994 was the first year in which it was possible to take full advantage of the opportunity, presented by legislation, to form sufficient reserves in accordance with Česká pojišt'ovna's strategic objective of achieving the standard level of capital and reserves in the European Union. This process was fully successful and Česká pojišt'ovna maintains a leading position in the Czech insurance market in the absolute majority of products offered.

The present position of the now fully privatised Česká pojišt'ovna is not only the result of the honest, hard work of all employees, agents, advisors and other cooperating companies, whose activities are essential for providing quality insurance services, but primarily as an extraordinary commitment to our customers and to the healthy development of the new Czech insurance market.

In response to growing customer needs in a market economy, Česká pojišt'ovna decided to gradually build up a financial group called Česká pojišt'ovna Group (CP-Group), which will enable financial and capital services to be provided to clients on an integrated basis. Along with the parent company, Česká pojišt'ovna a.s., CP-Group is formed by a variety of its major subsidiaries, including its daughter company in the Slovak Republic, Česká pojišt'ovna-Slovensko, a.s.

Česká pojišt'ovna a.s. is prepared to offer its customers the highest quality of insurance products and services to meet their needs, not only in the Czech Republic but also abroad in support of their international activities.

For further information interested parties should contact either Česká pojišt'ovna's Head Office in Prague or its representative office in London.

Česká pojišt'ovna a.s.
Head Office, Spalena 16
113 04 Praha 1
Tel: 42 2 2405 1225 Fax: 42 2 2424 1081

Česká pojišt'ovna a.s.
London Representative Office
9-13 Fenchurch Buildings
London EC3M 5HR
Tel: 0171 481 0041 Fax: 0171 481 1141

Tradition
Capital Strength
International
know-how

ČESKÁ POJIŠŤOVNA, a.s., Insurance and Reinsurance Corporation
Spálená 16, 113 04 Prague 11, Czech Republic,
Telephone: 0042 2 24 05 1 11, Fax: 0042 2 24 110 67
London Contact Office 9/13 Fenchurch Buildings, London EC3

8

Industrial Restructuring

John Waugh, PA Consulting Group

- Everyone's talking about the opportunities in Central and Eastern
  Europe and the need to get involved in the developments in the
  Czech Republic to provide a springboard into these opportunities.

- Industrial retsructuring is gathering pace in the Czech Republic and
  the opportunities should be exploited now – don't miss the boat!

Statements which, if accepted in isolation, would have the world
queueing up to buy into the 'action' here to the exclusion of other markets. There *are* opportunities. Some are strategically important in a
global context; most are fraught with difficulties which can make
exploitation unattractive.

This chapter focuses attention on the key issues which impact on the
scale and pace of industrial restructuring in the Czech Republic and
sets pointers for the British business person to consider in judging the
'opportunities' available.

Industrial restructuring in context

The phrase 'Industrial restructuring' can conjure up a variety of pic-
tures ranging from whole-scale reshaping of the industry base at
national level to rationalisation and development of single-site businesses. For the British industrialist who wants to do business in the
Czech Republic, it is more important to understand what the opportunities are in his sphere of activity in a 'local' sense, set within the
national context, and how to exploit them.

To do this it is important to understand something of the history of
Czech industry, its past strengths, and some of the developments which
have taken place in recent years. In addition it is important to know
something about the people, their education and culture, and the
impact of the changes which have taken place since 1989. From these
beginnings it is possible to appreciate more readily the type and scale
of opportunities available and the likely issues to be faced in trying to

exploit them. There is also a need to be clear in terms of the 'local' sense. Is it the intent to move into a complete industry sector, to build part of a 'global position'? Or is the focus the 'local' manufacturing business which can provide low-cost production of high value-added products to support his ailing facilities in the UK?

Whichever the driver, there are attractive opportunities for doing business with Czech enterprises to generate competitive advantage. Any opportunity will carry with it the need for some degree of industrial restructuring both within the Czech enterprises and their suppliers, customers, competitors and alliances.

Industrial restructuring, in the context of this chapter, will be viewed as the activity to change ownerships and intercompany relationships to create a new basis for competition.

Background

Understanding the past provides some rationale for the future. So, what and where is the Czech Republic? A 'young' country born of war and quiet revolution, set in the heart of Europe. It enjoyed a turbulent history as an integral part of the Holy Roman and Austro-Hungarian Empires before emerging, in 1918, as the dominant partner in the Czechoslovakian Federal Republic. Whilst most know Prague as the capital city, few know of the threat posed to its pre-eminent position in the middle ages by Kutná Hora, the once fabulously rich silver mining town. Now Kutná Hora boasts only the large Tabac factory, owned by Philip Morris, museums and tourist attractions. Nor will they know of Brno, where the Bren gun (the first UK and Czechoslovakian industrial joint venture, in 1918 – from BRno and ENfield) was made and Zetor tractors are still made and exported to the UK and Ireland.

These apart, this complex landscape was the setting for some of Europe's finest glass and crystal. Bohemian Crystal is well known around the world. However, less well known is the reputation Czech glass enjoyed over the last three hundred years. Czech glass is probably the only real competition to Murano glass from Venice – in terms of both quality and innovation, sometimes leading, sometimes following.

Manufacturing industry developed in all spheres between the wars to promote Czechoslovakia to fifth place in world industrial GDP per capita (this at a time when Britain was 10th or 12th). Czechoslovakia, particularly the Czech half, was an innovative and wealthy country and had a financial industry to match.

Education supported these developments, helping to build an engineering and processing excellence the equal of any country. Vast empires were built – in engineering, Škoda, ČKD, ZTS; steel manufacture in Košice, Vítkovice, Kladno and Třinec; armaments and ordnance in Brno, Vsetín, Česky Brod, Martin and Trenčín; jewellery in Jablonec and Liberec; textile machinery in Liberec and so on. Every facet of manufacturing and process industry was covered.

Whilst the war years took their toll, the introduction of Communism, in 1948, had a much more devastating effect. Gone was the competitive element, driving innovation and development. In came central planning and an increasingly bureaucratic and inefficient system of product allocations/quotas and failed delivery targets – to and from producers. Industrial restructuring at national level was seen, with much of the armaments industry moved to Slovakia. Investment lagged behind requirements to the point where most of the industry deteriorated to conditions far worse than in the 1950s. Rather than being efficient and productive, companies became employment centres. Motivation was stifled through inflexible salary gradings, lack of merit-based promotions and antipathy to innovation – technical or managerial.

Whilst the technical excellence of Czech engineering and science graduates was well respected, they enjoyed little freedom to express their talent. They were then, and still are today, the centre of excellence in the old 'East Bloc' – today's Central Europe. Now they provide the springboard for today's developments in the Czech economy and are eager to exploit their rediscovered freedom of expression.

The finance industry stagnated and recessed. Commercial and retail banking, as we know it in the West, did not develop. The capital markets and the insurance and pensions industries were virtually non-existent when Communism was overthrown in 1989. It was to be 1991–1993 before these were to enjoy a reawakening.

The pre-Communist past illustrated the entrepreneurial potential which was to survive the regime and provide the building blocks for today's developments.

Does the Czech Republic's re-emergence as a modernist economy have anything to offer?

Prague is closer to London than Vienna, 80 miles or so further west. Transportation to and from the country is improving rapidly as is the infrastructure within the country. Having split, quietly, from Slovakia at the end of 1992, the Czech Republic is the most Europe-oriented of the Central European countries. English is once again developing into the second language.

Where, then, are the opportunities and what are the issues to be faced when considering an investment into a Czech enterprise?

The first question to be addressed is 'why come here at all?' What are the objectives to be satisfied in developing business in Czech Republic? Are you interested in cheaper products, access to new markets, strengthening a global position? Obviously much depends on your type of business.

The financial services industry is key to the pace of change. The capital market freedoms introduced in the early 1990s enabled the voucher privatisation process to make a real impact on ownership. The freedoms, uncontrolled, led to an explosion in publicly tradeable shares, small shareholders, investment funds and brokers. Unfortunately, the majority of shares fell into the hands of a small number of investment funds, most of which are linked directly or indirectly to one or other of the major Czech banks. The bad news is that the banking sector is currently plagued with notable failures, non-performing loans and low interest rate margins. As if that was not enough, allegations of corruption, self dealing and secret trading have affected investor confidence, driving foreign investors to seek better returns in Warsaw and Budapest. Without reform and injections of new capital, the pace of change will stagnate.

Political divisiveness, power struggles and disagreements fostered a further lack of confidence that the reforms, so urgently required, will not be forthcoming. The Government's ownership of the largest stake in each of the four major banks and through them, their related investment funds and in its own right, its ownership of large stakes in Czech business and industry is stifling small investor interest. There are still too many barriers to bad-debt collection. The Czech Republic is still to experience it's first major bankruptcy.

Encouragingly, reforms are on their way. But slowly! The financial sector is providing opportunities for major foreign institutions. German, Austrian and French banks, investment funds and insurance companies are making inroads, forcing the pace of change of ownerships and relationships.

Privatisation has resulted in 70 per cent of GNP being realised in the private sector, with the majority of its exports going to EU and beyond rather than to the old COMECON countries. The Czech economy grew by 5 per cent in 1995 and is expected to perform at similar levels during 1996 and 1997. Inflation is below 9 per cent, wages have grown 35 per cent since 1992 and unemployment is below 3 per cent nationally.

The utilities can be seen to offer more of the same opportunities as at home, be it water, power, heat, telecommunications or gas – ownership and operating of assets and infrastructure. They offer the prospect of strategic expansion into an emerging and rapidly developing competitive market.

Retailing

The food and drinks industry offers the prospect of new markets and new products, many of which are exported to the UK or other parts of Europe. Major international players have already moved into the market through joint venture/aquisitions such as Nestle, Danone and Bass, whereas others are setting up greenfield operations.

The retail industry is a platform for expansion into a developing market with potentially higher margins than the increasingly competitive UK environment. Tesco, Marks & Spencer and Next are now present on the high street.

Manufacturing and process industries

Although the second and third waves of coupon privatisation led to the 'independence' from the State of much of the manufacturing base, and active trading on the newly opened Prague stock exchange, most still have some degree of direct or indirect State holding. There were obvious complications caused by the division of the Federal Republic into two separate states. Asset ownership was, and to a degree still is, a major issue.

With an increasing awareness of the competitive pressures to be faced in world markets, manufacturing industry is looking for opportunities to 'break out'. The major names of the past are still with us, Škoda, ČKD, Tesla, PAL, among others. These are fragmenting, to a degree, with subsidiaries gaining independence or being acquired by companies such as Ford, Lucas, Siemens, ABB. All of these were powerful manufacturing enterprises which still have strong capability, albeit with dated technologies and management practices.

The process industry appears to be moving in the opposite direction with increasing influence and acquisitiveness of groupings such as Chemapol, Chemapetrol and Spolchemie. These former trading enterprises are rapidly establishing major positions across the chemicals, pharmaceuticals and petrochemicals industry.

These industrial changes have brought with them an incresing awareness of the need for new ownership structures, supplier relationships, markets to access and the creation of alliances. The current environment, despite initial disappointments in dealing with potential foreign partners, is more confident and constructive. However, the legacy of uncontrolled development in capital markets lives on within the tangled web of ownership and influences one has to plough through in order to create a workable, profitable new industrial investment. However, with commitment and focus come the rewards.

Factors you should bear in mind before making any moves

Depending on the drivers you respond to in seeking opportunities within the Czech environment the following are generally applicable:

- Nothing happens quickly here, bureaucracy is an industry which keeps many employed.

- Czech companies still have highly fragmented ownership except for the very large and the very small.

- Ownership tends to be spread across investment funds, banks, the Fund of National Property and small share holders and finds representation in Boards of Directors, Supervisory Boards and Executive Management Teams.

- The funds and banks are attempting to focus their portfolios and, as a result, are seeking more influential shareholdings in their target companies, in some cases swapping stakes and ownerships.

- The Fund of National Property is under increasing pressure to sell its holdings and, at the same time, appears to be showing stronger nationalist tendencies.

- Most companies have sizeable debt, often as a result of uncollected/ uncollectable revenues from in-country or Eastern European (mainly Russian) customers.

- There is an urgent need for capital investment in the vast majority of enterprises.

- Cash management is poor, focus on shareholder value is almost non-existent and finance systems need realignment with UK, Euro or GAAP reporting procedures – as well as retaining their ability to satisfy Czech fiscal requirements.

- Overmanning is prevalent, between 30–100 per cent compared with the west; productivity is low and management practice weak, in services and producers.

- Customer focus is practically non-existent and supplier relationships are not measured and are in need of a radical overhaul.

- Wage rates are very low, but are starting to rise – 10–15 per cent pa is not uncommon.

- People are highly resistent to change, mainly because of poor communication, lack of understanding and commitment, lack of trust and weak leadership

In summary, there are opportunities and they can bring rewards – you have to understand how they can be exploited and whether the rewards meet your objectives.

On a larger scale industrial restructuring has developed opportunities within whole sectors. This is certainly starting to happen in the financial services, water, energy distribution (while power generation is not yet ready for privatisation), telecommunications, food and drink, retail, consumer durables/electronics, distribution, automotive and construction industries. In general/heavy engineering it is not so prevalent, although ABB is now a major player here. The same is true of the process industries which are still seeking suitors.

Whether the 'yet to arrive' or the 'already here' British industrialist will find this market attractive for first time or further investment is dependent on a variety of factors, including those listed above. A clear strategy is a prerequisite, as is the desire and ability to commit senior executive time and investment capital to the exercise from the outset. This must be constantly reappraised and reconfirmed.

Go to those who know the market for advice and guidance, whether professional advisors or businesses operating here already. They all have valuable experience. Bring bags of patience. You'll need it.

9

Business Management Culture

Michael Hermann, Anglo-Czechoslovak Ventures Ltd

Commuting between Prague and London I am often reminded of the Jewish father who, to complete his son's education, sent him to a Catholic church to observe the practice of another religion. Coming back the little boy reported, 'It was all very nice, music and incense, but the actual service was spoilt by a little urchin in a nightshirt who pinched the rabbi's hat and hid it. The rabbi looked right and left and knelt down to look under the table, but, of course, he couldn't read from the Torah without a hat. At last the boy in the nightshirt brought the hat back, but it was too late, the service was over.'

What strikes one is that well-meaning western experts, while observing correctly what is happening to the managerial strata in an ex-Communist country, do not always really understand what it means. Unavoidably, they put what they observe within the framework of their own very different experience. The same, of course, is true of the ex-Communist manager arriving in the West and trying to learn very quickly the managerial routines without knowing the frame of reference within which alone they can be understood.

In my experience, western misconceptions about Czech business and its management come under three headings:

1. The management needs to operate as a western business enterprise in a market economy.

2. The narrowness of their perspective results from insufficient education and knowledge.

3. When they are in managerial positions and have been there for some considerable time, they must know the basics about profit margins, marketing and keeping a diary of appointments.

Background to business mentality

In spite of the profusion of new legislation and the even greater profusion of political speeches about the transition to a market economy, and in spite of the real moves towards privatisation, the Czech managers do not operate in a free market competitive economy and the survival of their businesses – I am talking now only about medium to large enterprises – does not entirely depend on making profit or even remaining solvent. The problems they face are mostly macroeconomic, which even the best managers cannot solve by their own means.

As far as big industry and distributive organisations are concerned, the first step towards privatisation was the turning of 'National enterprises' into joint stock companies, followed by the now-famous voucher privatisation.

Privatisation of small businesses, shops and restaurants has been real. As far as medium and large enterprises are concerned, the distribution of shares through vouchers, received by each adult resident for free, often had little effect on the management. The optimistic view is that the transfer of shares into the hands of a few investment funds will continue in the form of Unit Funds or Investment Trusts, and that these will keep the management on their toes. British experience with the influence exercised by investment and pension funds on companies in which they have significant equity participation does not really augur well but perhaps the Czech Republic will fare better, because the number of quoted companies, as well as that of the investment funds, will be much smaller. This means that the supervision of management will be more necessary for funds holding bigger blocks of shares and also will be easier to exercise because of the smaller number of players.

Privatisation has had a greater and faster effect on the transformation of national enterprises into business concerns where it is effected by the participation of a foreign company. Although foreign partners encountered some problems, of which I will mention only two, with hindsight most of them judge their investment worthwhile.

Firstly the higher level of salaries paid to western expatriates is not likely to convince the lesser paid Czech managerial staff that they should be as efficient as the foreign manager. Secondly, the mentality of the workforce, developed over years when no one could be fired and when industrial action was illegal and now with the added disincentive of very low unemployment, means that there is great pressure for salary increases without a corresponding rise in productivity. In areas where unemployment dictates that low wages are accepted as an unchangeable fact of life, individuals seek additional income in moonlighting.

When the German manager of the Volkswagen-Skoda works spoke about his experiences, soon after being appointed, he was surprised by the high technological standard and equipment of the Czech factories. He was even more surprised by the very high degree of skill shown by the Czech workers. His problem was that as a result of established working practices, he needed four workers to do a job which was done by only one in Germany.

As individuals are well educated and highly skilled, these internal problems facing a manager are not insoluble. Further, high individual motivation is commonplace. However, in many instances there is no corresponding corporate financial pressure. It is not easy for the manager to confront politically and socially unpopular issues when there is no threat of insolvency. The Czech Republic enacted an insolvency law, which allows to bring into bankruptcy enterprises where the total of debts is higher than the total of claims against other enterprises – never mind that the claims they have are against enterprises equally insolvent as they are. To find the beginning of the chain of insolvencies and to help by re-financing the culprit at the beginning of the chain is an extremely difficult and slow process. The wholesale elimination of insolvent enterprises has been postponed indefinitely and one can well understand why: to close down all enterprises which are insolvent would mean shutting down large parts of Czech industry.

Solvency problems are not the only and possibly not the most important problems of the Czech manager. To break down well established industry structures takes time and the persisting monopolisation of sectors of the economy is often management's greatest obstacle. Monopolistic or oligopolistic national enterprises were converted into joint stock companies with the same market dominance and things got much worse after the liberalisation of prices. Monopolistic distribution organisations could increase substantially their wholesale and retail prices without increasing the prices they paid to the producers or the processing industry. The Czech manager, squeezed between a monopolistic supplier of materials or semi-products and a monopolistic distributor of his own product, is slowly getting used to the idea that political and governmental help to solve his problems is unlikely to come and that he can only be saved by making his own business more efficient.

Finally, one has to take into account that the 'Establishment Mafia', which controlled individual enterprises and whole branches of industry, often continue under the guise of new managements. Indeed, many apparatchiks and secret police officials, who could secure privileged positions in the past by brutal coercion, have quickly learned to achieve the same results in the form of a managerial mafia. In this connection the relatively low purchasing power of the Czech crown, the simultaneous existence of low salaried managers and government officials and of the affluent small businesses leads to a substantial increase in bribery and corruption, evading cumbersome regulations and bureaucratic constraints, and has often become an accepted form of doing business.

Education

A visiting western partner, separated from those with whom he does business by the barrier of language, sometimes jumps to the conclusion that Czechs lack proper education. A British or an American individual is more likely to make this mistake than a German or Austrian who went through an almost identical system of education as the Czechs. The Czech education system is fairly rigid, with a national curriculum for schools of all types and open to all without distinction of class or income. The primary and secondary schools insist on a level of discipline long abandoned in the English speaking countries. There is no question that people could leave a primary school without being able to write and count. The secondary schools have a much wider programme than British secondary schools so that in scientific subjects students reaching the universities already know what first year British university students have yet to learn. The universities, in their turn, are much more vocationally orientated than British universities and their courses take much longer; on average five years. A graduate degree is considered vocational specialisation; it is unlikely that a Czech language graduate would end up as a merchant banker.

It is a very thorough system with heavy emphasis on knowledge, sometimes criticised because it neglects to teach the students how to find what they need to know in source material and how to choose between different opinions of the authorities, unlike the best British schools and universities.

One can therefore assume that a Czech manager will have a much more comprehensive knowledge covering the natural as well as the social sciences, but that he will be less able than his British counterpart to source material and to assess it critically. This presents a certain problem for British managers, particularly those involved in joint ventures. The British manager relies on methods while the Czech prefers a concentration of facts and procedures to follow.

Lack of skills or courage?

There is a clear difference in attitudes and behaviour. Speaking to a number of western consultants called upon to advise and train Czech managers, who have sometimes been in managerial positions at a fairly high level and for many years, it is clear that they often assume that the individual must have at least the routine skills and a minimum of decisiveness required for such positions in the west. However, this is not necessarily the case.

A western businessman/woman trying to arrange his agenda will often be surprised that the Czech managers are unwilling or at least unaccustomed to making appointments for a couple of weeks ahead, while they are quite willing to see their visitors almost immediately or after a telephone call in the morning.

This is not necessarily a consequence of a Communist economy alone. In many western small cities where the number of players is small and the distance between the offices slight, the same habits exist. In the Czech Republic they were made worse by the fact that all the lines of command led to the centre and as long as the manager maintained contact with his superior and his own subordinates, the horizontal lines of communication did not really matter much.

The other, even more curious, phenomenon is the willingness to go and sit in meetings without expectation of any results. Projects are discussed, but their realisation seems to be other people's business. Promises are easily given and are often an expression of a friendly attitude, rather than of real intentions. To refuse or not commit to something, many Czech managers think, will be taken for hostility, while the failure to keep the promise can always be explained by circumstances over which the promisor has no control.

Such behaviour, which is an innate part of the cultural characteristic of the country, springs partly from the recent past experience and the deep-seated feelings that one can discuss projects, but that decisions will be taken by those above or by anonymous people in the organisation's apparatus.

In the case of most managers' experience (those older than 25–30 years) in the past the manager's job was to obey without question, and his income depended on his ability to please his taskmasters, who did not care about profitability or economy of production. Careers depended on finding a suitable niche in a suitable institution and climbing the ladder by pleasing the party bosses.

The transition to market economy was perceived by many of these managers as an opportunity to oust other managers, more tainted by their subservience to the Communist regime or – in the case of the more enterprising – to create for themselves new companies or institutions. The requirement of profitability is accepted as the new theory but taken by many no more seriously than Stalin's economics of socialism. Instead of Marx and Lenin, the reformed manager is likely to quote from Milton Friedman and Friedrich von Hayek, but in his heart of hearts he expects, naturally, to 'manage' very much as before, though he would never admit this, not even to himself.

To sum up this painful chapter: what the business manager needs in order to be successful in the Czech Republic is to learn how to manage enterprises while trying to survive not in a market economy but in the uncertainty of transition where political skills and contacts matter more than cash flow, remembering that the effort is worthwhile.

Part 2

Market Potential

10

Consumer Goods and Distribution

Deidre MacBean, Prague Associate of Cerrex Ltd

Although many UK exporters missed out on early opportunities and now face greater competition in the market, at least in terms of distribution, their task is far easier than that faced by those who entered the market immediately after the 1989 revolution. Whereas in 1990 an exporter had to find a distributor from a chaotic mass of wholesalers – none with national coverage and some with a distinctly cowboy approach – now some clear market leaders have emerged. In drinks, food, cosmetics and druggists' goods, international retailers such as Delhaize or manufacturers such as Unilever have supported the development and success of promising wholesalers and distributors at the expense of the less effective. Distribution in consumer electronics, clothing and footwear lags somewhat behind but should improve as retail chains begin to appear.

But how are the British doing in this increasingly sophisticated market? If Czechs are asked to name British products on sale in the Czech Republic, they will probably come up with cars such as Rolls Royce and Jaguar, drinks such as Guinness and Scotch Whisky, and perhaps people from Prague might know Mappin and Webb or Aquascutum and Pringles. Beyond that, few will be able to go. British impact on the Czech market since the revolution has, at least in the public consciousness, been limited to niche markets – while German, Italian and American imports have dominated the middle ground. The second half of the nineties should, however, see a rise in awareness of Britain's strengths with the arrival of three of the UK's biggest retailers – Marks & Spencer, Tesco and Next.

But while British retailing may be about to take off, where are the opportunities for the exporter?

Goods for the growing middle class have great potential. Home furnishings, DIY products – where a very promising market is developing

– street fashion, designer clothes, ready-made food, cosmetics and home electronics are all sectors where demand is increasing and becoming more sophisticated as incomes rise. Outlets for these products are growing and specialised media for their promotion abound. The exporter's task will be to persuade potential distributors not only that British reputation for quality and good service still holds, but also that 'British-made' means excellent value, high fashion and up-to-the-minute design as well.

The market

The Czech Republic is now in many ways as sophisticated as most western markets and, while price is still key, fierce competition makes quality, innovation and promotional support just as important. It takes something quite special to tempt Czech retailers or wholesalers to change suppliers or take on a new range.

Consumer goods is one of the most developed market sectors. In Prague, for instance, visitors are often surprised that they can buy the same brands they buy at home – sometimes, if they are lucky, with labels still in their original language. Drugstore shelves are filled with the familiar washing powders, face creams, hair sprays and baby lotions; newsstands carry Czech versions of international glossy magazines; anything from Guinness to Malibu is available in bars; the same jeans are piled on the clothes shops' shelves; and the same designer clothes hang in the exclusive boutiques. In short, everything looks – and unfortunately for the locals, mostly costs – much the same as back home.

But that is just a 'snap-shot' view. People who stay longer, and travel outside Prague, soon see the complete – not quite so rosy – picture. For instance, if they linger a few weeks, they may realise that even in the capital's top department stores, it is often best to stock up on their favourite products because they can disappear from the shelves just as suddenly as they once appeared. If they ventured further afield, to Northern Moravia for example, they might find that a request for a Coke would produce something bearing very little resemblance to the world-renowned product.

And it would soon dawn on any persistent traveller that, apart from a few exceptions such as the rapidly growing networks of petrol stations, there are very few local or international retail chains (eg record shops, drugstores, pharmacies, DIY shops, supermarkets or department stores) with recognisable branding, consistent layout, good presentation, regular promotion. Instead, coverage – even by the biggest Czech chains or internationals such as Plus discount (Tengelmann), Delvita (Delhaize) and Kmart (now Tesco) – is often only regional, around Prague, Brno or the Austrian or German borders. Outside these concentrations, many towns exhibit a hotchpotch of often crumbling, independent department stores, supermarkets and small, family-run 'drogerie' (drugstores), 'potraviny' (an equivalent of UK corner stores), 'textil' (clothing) and 'elektro' (consumer electronics).

The lack of large buying groups with national coverage has forced manufacturers of consumer goods – whether international or Czech – to patch together a number of distribution routes to get their goods to the customers. It has meant dealing with a few rare wholesalers with national coverage and a network of regional wholesalers, specialising in particular goods and in the kind of outlets they supply. Some wholesalers have built up good relations with the largest supermarkets and department stores, others with chains of petrol station shops and the rest with 'cash and carries', discount stores and the thousands of small independent retailers. The largest may import directly while others simply distribute.

Wholesalers' competence, solvency and experience vary drastically – and complacency is a problem frequently cited by manufacturers distributing through them. To fill in the gaps left by wholesalers, most large manufacturers have created and trained their own sales teams. Their role is also tactfully to encourage distributors and retailers to bring merchandising and stock control up to scratch.

Expected future trends

This chaotic situation is, however, likely to improve as soon as the leading wholesalers and retailers – multinational and Czech alike – consolidate their positions and expand. The day of the small trader looks numbered as the share of firms with less than 25 employees in the Czech Republic's trading turnover has fallen from two-thirds to less than half in the last three years and will surely fall much further.

Supermarkets

The European supermarket multiples which so far appear sparsely in the Czech Republic all have plans for expansion to reach national coverage. For example, Delvita, which currently has around 20 Prague-based stores, is building a new distribution centre and hopes by the year 2000 to have created a network of 80 stores around the Republic; Euronova (daughter company of the Dutch Ahold), currently in the top five supermarket groups operating in the Czech Republic, also has its own distribution centre and hopes to expand its network of grocery and drugstore discount stores and MANA supermarkets;

Rewe, the German group, is rumoured to be planning an assault on the market soon.

Foreign independents and Czech supermarket giants, which were quick to snap up as much of the former state chains as possible, are fighting the multinational onslaught through the formation of the Czech Marketing Distribution (CMD) company, quarter-owned by the Swiss-based European Marketing Distribution alliance. The aim of the seven-strong CMD is to concentrate buying to obtain better deals and to share marketing costs. One of the members, German-independent GLOBUS, is pioneering the first hypermarket in the Czech Republic – outside Brno, in Southern Moravia, its 100,000 square metre surface will house a supermarket, drugstore, and shops selling records, clothes, shoes, glass, porcelain, household goods and consumer electronics.

Household

On the household and DIY side, international players such as IKEA and the German retailers OBI and Baumax are all taking advantage of a boom in the home improvement market. In Prague, IKEA is moving to larger premises to allow it to introduce its internationally-known concept in its entirety and it also plans to open a second centre in Brno. OBI and Baumax both have a handful of hangar-size DIY stores in the outskirts of Prague or other major cities and have pioneered the concept of weekend shopping by car. Both plan quick expansions – but it may take some time before they persuade the experienced Czech DIY expert to swallow their prices, which can be up to three times as high as buying from the local ironmongers'.

Department stores

Networks of generalist department stores, selling food, clothes, sports goods, haberdashery, household goods and consumer electronics have been much slower to develop. The largest chain of this type was bought in April 1996 by Tesco from the American Kmart chain. It remains to be seen whether Tesco will change the store's range. The largest Prague department store, Kotva, which is directed towards middle to high income groups, plans dramatic expansion to build a nationwide chain of smaller stores stocking sports goods, fabrics and designer clothing. The imminent arrival of Marks and Spencer through a franchise arrangement will increase the competition in this area and opportunities for UK suppliers.

Pharmacies

Drugstore and pharmacy chains have not yet developed and cosmetics are sold mainly through dealers and specialised wholesalers (from high-class exclusive to mass market) who supply department stores and small independent drugstores, pharmacists and cosmetics shops. Rossman, the Austrian drugstore company with a couple of shops in Prague, has announced plans to build 60 Czech outlets over the next two years. Most of the luxury chains, such as Estee Lauder and Lancome, have established high-class Prague retail outlets and will probably expand to other cities as purchasing power grows.

Consumer electronics

No 'Dixons'-type chain yet exists in the Czech Republic and most of the turnover in consumer electronics, outside Tesco, is still through the thousands of small family-run 'elektros'. These are supplied by a few strong wholesalers as well as representatives of those international manufacturers who have set up local representatives and/or companies. British-run wholesaler DATART, one of the largest traders in the Czech Republic and distributor for TDK and Kenwood, already has several retail outlets in Prague and is looking for a foreign partner to help build up a national chain.

From the point of view of the consumer goods manufacturer, then, the situation in the Czech Republic looks promising. While competition will certainly grow, so will the number of good quality outlets through which customers can be reached. To succeed, companies will need a strong presence in the Czech Republic and make sure that it is *their* products which fill the shelves and not those of their competitors. And they will need to grasp the fact that the Czech market is increasingly sophisticated; Czech consumers will not settle for second best or goods that are considered in western Europe to be outdated.

EVERY **minute**
EVERY **hour**
EVERY **day**
we keep people
connected

EXPORT GUARANTEE
AND INSURANCE CORPORATION

Janovského 2, 170 32 Prague 7, Czech Republic
Telephone: 42/02/2014 1111

Pavol Parizek, General Manager

Introducing EGAP

EGAP - Export Guarantee and Insurance Corporation (in Czech Exportní garanční a pojišťovací společnost a.s.) is specializing in insurance of credit risks related to the export of goods and services from the Czech Republic. EGAP offers its insurance services to all exporters registered in the Czech Republic.

EGAP protects from the risks of default by the foreign buyer caused by the buyer himself or by political, financial or macro-economic situation of the buyer's country.

EGAP was founded in June 1992 as a fully state-owned joint-stock company with the present capital stock of CZK 1.3 billion.

EGAP operates under the Act No. 58/1995 Coll., on Insurance and Financing of Export with State Support, on the basis of which the Czech Republic guarantees the obligation of EGAP resulting from Insurance Policies.

EGAP offers insurance products similar in structure, extent and quality to those of established foreign Export Credit Agencies and is governed by the same rules which are effective for export credit and political risk insurance within the European Union and OECD.

EGAP is a member of the International Union of Credit and Investment Insurers - the Berne Union with an Observer status. Subsequent to the membership of the Czech Republic in OECD, EGAP was appointed as the Czech Republic's representative in the Group on Export Credits and Credit Guarantees.

Payment Risks Connected With Foreign Buyers and Covered by EGAP Insurance

Payment Risks Can Be Divided Into Two Main Groups:

Political risks endanger the collection of foreign receivables of Czech exporters; these risks result from political, financial or macro-economic situation of the foreign buyer's country, or possibly of a third country, and are considered as force majeur by the both business partners. These risks include, above all:

- **political events** in the buyer's country, such as international or civil war, revolution, uprising, civil unrest, strikes etc, which result in payment difficulties.

- **possibility to transfer payments to the Czech Republic** in consequence of serious economic difficulties occurring in the buyer's country, declaration of insolvency of this country, introduction of a moratorium on payments or introduction of foreign-exchange regulations restricting transfer of payments.

- **administrative decisions of state authorities in the buyer's country** which prevent execution of the contract or transfer of payments from the contract (e.g. withdrawal of import or export licence, cancellation or withdrawal of previously issued permits necessary for execution of the contract, freezing of deposits etc.).

- **administrative and political measures in third countries** through which payments are effected that prevent transfer of payments to the Czech Republic (e.g. embargo or restrictions of transfer payments etc.).

- **natural disasters** in consequence of which non-payment of financial obligations occurs through no fault of the buyer.

- **non-payment by a foreign buyer, who is a public sector entity, is considered to be a political risk.**

Commercial risks arise directly from the economic and financial situation of the foreign buyer. These are:

- **proven insolvency** of the foreign buyer evidenced by the court decision documenting the bankruptcy proceedings against the buyer who is a private entity and subject to bankruptcy proceedings.

- **presumed insolvency or unwillingness** of the foreign buyer to fulfil obligations arising from the contract which is evidenced by his failure to pay the debt even after the waiting period set in the insurance policy (protracted default).

Insurance claim may occur, however, only outside the territory of the Czech Republic and only if the exporter has fulfilled all provisions of the contract, above all quantity and quality of contractual deliveries and delivery deadlines.

In most cases EGAP insures a combination of commercial and political risks.

11

Grocery Retailing

Michael Prokop, Prokop International Ltd

Introduction

The Czech Republic is considered in many areas to be in the forefront of the former Eastern European countries. It is attracting foreign investment, it has the lowest inflation and one of the highest disposable incomes – yet as far as the grocery market is concerned it is far behind other Eastern European countries. Will the entry of Tesco and Marks and Spencer wake up the market? Are the manufacturers and importers getting a good deal and are their sales teams ready for the inevitable changes in the pattern of distribution?

To a superficial observer the grocery and FMCG markets in the Czech republic have not made any visible progress over the last three years. Indeed, since privatisation in the early 1990s the marketplace looks very much the same. The big local chains such as Interkontakt Group and M-Holding are just a collection of old state shops with no branding/image of their own – same shop trading under different facia. In many cases these shops survive because they have a mini monopoly in a given area and when an aggressive retailer opens in their vicinity they suffer. True – the big international multiples such as Euronova (Ahold), Delvita or Plus-Discount (Tengelmann) are increasing the number of outlets and their market share, but as at 1995 only one supermarket group – the wholly Czech owned Interkontakt Group – exceeded 2 per cent market share; all other groups have below one per cent market share based on their declared turnover.

Foreign investors

The big plans of the foreign players in the early 1990s have not taken place for a variety of reasons:

1. The availability of green field sites in the major conurbations is limited, the planning process is cumbersome and in many cases dependent upon the whims of local government clerks.

2. The lack of availability of skilled and trustworthy management material to run the stores is preventing the confidence to make a major commitment.

3. The shopping pattern is still taking time to change. Prior to 1989 the customer had to visit several shops to do his/her daily shopping – so purchases were small in volume and in value – and the old habits are dying hard. The use of credit cards in a super-market context is almost unknown and so it is payment in cash, which is in turn dependent on payday – so the expenditure curve goes up around the 10th day of each month. Use of cars is now increasing so there is no physical barrier to getting the shopping home in bulk, but the use of big deep freezers is limited due to the small kitchens built in the traditional concrete town flats.

So why – in comparison – have the neighbouring countries such as Poland and Hungary had a much faster development of the grocery market? One of the reasons lies in the inheritance of the Communist era which was far more draconian in the then Czechoslovakia, when no private enterprise was allowed, as against the more pragmatic attitude in the neighbouring countries. But this head start is not the only reason. The major problem seems to be the planning process which offers little incentive for the local councils to attract new business and investment into the area. With unemployment of less than 2 per cent in many major conurbations, the signals experienced in Hungary and Poland have not been registered as yet. The recent departure of the French giant Auchan from the Czech market is also significant – they have been unsuccessfully negotiating for two years for a hypermarket site on the outskirts of Prague – and their accusations of a need of bribery to do business in the Czech republic have left a bitter taste on both sides. In fact, Auchan have promptly turned their sights on Portugal and the local chain Pa'o de Ac'ucar (Sugar Loaf) – perhaps a 'jilted bride' reaction.

So while, for example, in Poland the Makro Cash and Carry group have over 6 per cent market share and in Hungary a joint venture part-nered by J. Mainl from Austria has almost 6 per cent or Tengelmann's local company has almost 5 per cent of the market, in the Czech market we are still waiting for the first true hypermarket to open.

The state of the market reminds me of the situation in Portugal in the late 1980s when the small- to medium-sized stores dominated the market until the French chain Continent opened their first major out-let in Lisbon, followed shortly by one in Oporto. Perhaps such a cata-lyst is what the market needs – to prove to itself that, despite the above drawbacks, there is a major opportunity in providing – under one roof – the 'complete shopping experience'.

Local issues

Local manufacturers and importers, meanwhile, have the worst of all possible worlds. They are increasingly pressurised by chains – both domestic and international – for payment terms and discounts based on a sophisticated, central warehouse driven pattern of distribution, but are in turn offered no major benefits. So individual branch delivery is still the customary mode of goods distribution and a sales person's call is still required to order the goods. Some chains are trying to circumvent the sales person's calls but often this leads to out-of-stock situations as the store staff do not have the ability or the mechanisms to ensure proper stock control. Again, a major reason is the low quality of the store personnel – usually due to the artificially low unemployment rates in many areas. The quality of salespeople varies tremendously from company to company – mainly dependent on the quality of, and investment into, sales training. Many companies are realising that with no sales heritage over the last 40 years they have to start from zero – and in many cases from minus – just to instil some of the basic commercial attributes such as assertivity, decision-making skills and desire for excellence. The average sales person is young – probably early 20s – and so in addition the maturity is also lacking. However, that is often replaced by enthusiasm and willingness to perform mundane tasks such as merchandising as an integral (and major) part of their job.

The function of a sales person is well rewarded – on average after two years a good sales person will earn twice the national average wage – and that can still be in their early 20's. Nevertheless there is still a shortage of good sales people – precisely because it is such a new profession which commenced its life in early 1990's. Sales management is recruited from the ranks of experienced sales staff which is no guarantee of a good manager and the directors of sales and marketing are still in many instances expatriates. A good local sales manager is worth their weight in gold – perhaps only eclipsed in worth by a good local financial manager.

Summary

Despite all the above caveats the market is successful, both manufacturers and retailers are making money and those who understand the market have built good, solid businesses. The purchase of Kmart branches in the Czech Republic (and Slovakia) by Tesco could be just the signal the market is waiting for. Their experience in running hypermarkets and bias towards grocery should inject new impetus into the marketplace.

The old Kmart setup, which was created by the purchase of some of the state owned Prior department stores gives them a good base, with almost 1 per cent market share from only a few sites. Let us also hope that Marks and Spencer with their first branch in Prague will not only provide the Czech customers with quality non-food items but in time also grocery and chilled, freshly made food – one segment completely missing from the Czech supermarket due to the poor existing logistical skills. When I am able to buy a fresh chilled Chicken Kiev in a provincial town – then I will know that the market has matured.

12

Food Processing

Cerrex Ltd

It is estimated that in the Czech Republic, food processing, which employs about 120 000 people, accounted for some 15 per cent of GNP in 1994–5. Retail sales of food in 1995 accounted for some CZK 230 billion.

The Czech government has been very successful in encouraging foreign investment into the food processing sector. A number of branches within the sector, including beer (which includes malt and Moravian barley), spirits, sugar, sausages, dairy products (including yoghurt and natural cheeses) have traditionally had a very high reputation and, together with tobacco, confectionery, vegetable oils and fats, bakery products, slaughterhouses and sugar refineries, have been among the most profitable. These were not as badly affected by the disintegration of Eastern markets as most other industrial sectors in the country. In the future, there are expected to be good prospects for the new technologies of low calorie food production, frozen products, various ready-made meals, fast foods, yoghurts and fresh cheeses. We would expect to see the development of out-of-town supermarkets equipped with modern technology. Consumers have gradually benefited from a much wider assortment of products, higher quality food products and better services in supermarkets established by foreign firms.

Food processing was traditionally characterised by inefficiencies in the supply chain and a high level of wastage caused by poor food collection, processing shortages and poor distribution (although in these respects the Czech Republic has been better than almost all others in Central Europe). This led to inconsistency of food supply and generally low quality foodstuffs with a short shelf life. After 1989, with the opening of the market to imports and consumer preferences for fresh goods rather than tinned foodstuffs, there has been a fall in the demand for locally produced canned fruit and vegetable products, skimmed milks and butter.

The Czechs realise that to survive in the competitive western markets they have to improve packaging and bottling, adhere to western standards, improve marketing and modernise production technology in a number of sectors, especially with regard to sausages and sugar.

The picture for the industry is improving as the Czechs achieve greater penetration in foreign markets in beer, processed meat and dairy products; improve processing, packaging and plastic wrapping and are steadily winning back their own domestic market. The Czechs say that all (105 in total) dairy plants in the Czech Republic meet both Czech and EU hygiene standards. Since 1994 the Czechs have been taking on board EU standards on packaging and labelling, consumer protection and health safeguards, and firms are encouraged to meet ISO 9000.

In order to reduce the high energy bills the manufacture of cans is being oriented towards more easily opened shapes and profiles, the introduction of high quality varnished and two-part cans. Major increases have taken place in the use of aluminium foil, polypropylene wrapping and boiling bags and the use of tough polystyrene. The introduction of foreign food chains in the Czech Republic has, however, proved of little help to the Czech industry, as they have tended to source products from outside the country. Also, because of a shortage of domestic capital, the Czechs find it difficult to establish their own major outlets.

Major foreign purchases have included the takeover of Ceske Cokoladovny by Nestlé and BSN, Philip Morris's purchase of part of the Czech Tabak Co., Norwegian interests, through investment in Vitona (which now appears to account for some 65 per cent of the total soup market), and Heinz, through its investment in the production of dairy products, infant foodstuffs, and powdered milk. The most well-publicised UK purchase has been the Bass investment in Prague Breweries, Prazske Pivovary, although the Czechs have always been in two minds about the extent to which they wish to encourage foreign investment in the brewery industry.

The Czechs have already had a strong presence in the aluminium foil and tube sectors. PAP, with foreign investment, now meets 80 per cent of demand for paper and plastic cups, yoghurt cartons and other jars. Austrian and US investment has been directed towards the modernisation of meat processing and freezing, packaging and improved marketing. Swiss investment has gone into a new corrugated cardboard plant in Nymburk, industrial bottling equipment, improved freezer capacities and modern energy generation. Chovosil, the food packaging manufacturers, have extended their lines to include foil printing equipment, cellophane polypropylene and polyethylene foils. Confidence is such that McDonalds now reportedly buy 80 per cent of their food packaging and products from Czech companies. PKL aims for 25 per cent of the filling machines and cardboard drinks markets and Gamex, formerly a leading office equipment supplier, has moved into packaging for milk and meat products with 60 per cent investment from Viscofin (Spain).

13

Energy

Cerrex Ltd*

Introduction

Due to its tight political and economic links with the Soviet Union the Czech economy was geared to an extensive development of high-energy and materials-intensive sectors. Since that era the government has moved significantly towards market pricing of energy products, reduced state subsidies and privatised state-owned enterprises. Progress has been retarded however in some areas by political concerns about the social impact of greatly increased domestic fuel prices and higher unemployment arising from imposing further costs on some already uncompetitive industries.

It is recognised, however, that further progress in the energy sector generally is central to sustaining the momentum of the transition of the whole economy away from its market-insulated intensive use, sole supply energy legacy of central planning.

Progress is also being influenced by the heavy role the energy sector has occupied in polluting the environment and the consequent impact on it of environmental legislation being introduced by the newly formed Environmental Ministry. Pollution controls are being placed on the preponderance of coal-fired power plants and others are being closed as new nuclear power plants completed with western assistance become available. Projects to link up with European pipelines and power grids are also well advanced, with the involvement of several European consortia.

The energy scene

The legacy of central planning cannot be eliminated in the short term and some measures being planned are aimed at longer term objectives of achieving a more balanced energy mix than currently exists. The country is relatively poor in energy resources. Coal, especially low

---

*Staff of Cerrex Ltd act as advisors to the Czech government on energy matters.

grade high sulphur lignite, dominates domestic energy production and accounts for 40 per cent of energy needs. There is virtually no oil and gas production and a limited amount of hydropower.

Approximately 35 per cent of all energy needed is imported and the former Soviet Union still supplies nearly all oil and gas used. Older generation nuclear power stations provide some additional electricity supply but pose problems in meeting internationally accepted standards.

Overall energy demand has fallen sharply since 1989 due to Comecon trade collapsing and large-scale industrial restructuring, impacting heavily on many industries unable to compete in a free market environment. Recent statistics indicate that some growth is occurring in gas and electricity use, particularly in the residential sector. Cerrex would comment, however, that this is somewhat deceptive as it includes continuing support for direct state subsidies (district heat) and cross subsidies (for gas and electricity) that protect household consumers. Transport sector demand is growing but has yet to reach levels comparable with that in developed western economies.

The breakup of the Czech and Slovak Federal Republic has had little impact on the energy sector as the two countries already possessed separate electricity companies, oil refineries, oil and gas distribution companies and marketing operations. Two company arrangements have been established and appear to be collaborating effectively in managing the Friendship and Brotherhood pipelines from Russia and the Ukraine and the Adria pipeline from the Croatian coast and on which both countries are largely dependent for fuel supplies.

Energy production

Electricity

The Czech Republic retains a sophisticated power system, serving as a major supplier of electricity in central Europe. The predominant electricity producer CEZ has a generating capacity in excess of 11 000 mw, currently consisting of the Dukovany nuclear power plant, ten fossil fuel plants and numerous hydroelectric plants. Although semi-privatised in the form of a joint stock company (with government control), government policy allowing CEZ to operate as an integrated generation-transmission company is seen by many observers of the Czech scene as a negative in the development of a competitive power sector in view of CEZ's virtual monopoly position.

The sector as a whole is investing heavily in pollution control equipment on all large coal-fired power plants but is hampered in raising the requisite finance by the still too low tariff structure allowed by the government. While CEZ is fairly well off financially other energy supply companies, particularly the distributors, are finding increasing problems in financing rehabilitation of the transmission and distribution systems.

District heating

Over 30 per cent of the country's population is served by district heating. Much of this is based on inefficient, relatively old district heating and industrial cogenerating plants. Most of the plants use low quality coal or heavy fuel oil. The government is encouraging the upgrading of these schemes and many western equipment manufacturers and consultants have been closely involved in this, often with support from international aid bodies including the EU. The use of natural gas is seen as a cost-effective method of meeting the stricter pollution control standards. Western technology based on this is now heavily promoted both at the regional and local administrative levels of government, and in the increasingly privately owned district heating sectors. Many observers such as Cerrex, with first-hand experience of the sector, see the year 2000 as the crunch point. This is when subsidies for heat are targeted to be finally removed, and will concentrate consumers' minds greatly on energy savings at the point of use and the relative efficiency of the delivery system *vis à vis* other competing forms of supply.

Oil

The disintegration of the Soviet Union and the CMEA disrupted traditional trade flows including vital supplies of crude oil. The closure of the Adria oil pipeline link to the Mediterranean due to the war in the former Yugoslavia exacerbated the situation. The country's dependence on crude oil supplies from Russia and the Ukraine is still high and in order to lessen dependency the government is investing in new pipelines, including a 340km line connecting the transalpine pipeline (TAP) at Ingolstadt to the main refineries at Kralupy and Litvinov. The scope for such diversification is, however, relatively small and expensive, indicating that the existing supply pattern is likely to remain for the foreseeable future.

A particular problem being faced is the lack of crude oil storage capacity required to replace the previous predictable supply from the Soviet Union through the supply pipelines. Since the separation of the Czech and Slovak Republics the only significant crude oil storage capacity is at the refineries, leaving the economy vulnerable to oil supply shocks. Overall it is estimated that the country has only about 12 days' supply compared with 30 days' operational storage in most OECD countries.

Natural gas

The Czech Republic is located at the crossroads of the main pipeline system delivering Russian gas to western Europe and will continue to benefit financially from gas transit fees. Natural gas is forecast to play an increasingly important role in the energy sector and is already replacing small scale coal use in urban areas. Much of the large growth is in the conversion of heating plants in industry and municipal district heating. An important element affecting further conversion and new project development is the price level which is planned to rise to market levels as various official subsidies are withdrawn. An increase in price levels is also necessary for the eight regional distribution companies to finance expansion of existing networks which are inadequate to meet existing geographical demand and to upgrade the antiquated metering systems and other similar investments. At present price levels, such investments are barely economic, although the position has improved (since 1993) from being totally uneconomic.

Coal

Czech coal reserves, despite their considerable size, are not suited to mining expansion for economic and environmental reasons. The present domestic demand for lignite is strongly influenced by heating plants, industry and small general users. Use of lignite for power generation, which in western countries accounts for almost all its use, amounts to only about 50 per cent of lignite consumption in the Czech Republic. Present policies of the government are to phase out lignite consumption in all non-power markets in support of its environmental protection and energy efficiency programmes. Progress in this is, however, as in other sectors of the economy, slower than might be desirable as the government seeks to keep down the level of unemployment in the country.

The resultant restructuring is forcing a concentration and consolidation among the 20 or so independent coal distributors and newly privatised coal mining companies. Forecasts are that a viable industry will emerge, producing approximately 30m tons of lignite (1994: 60m); five million tons of hard coal (1994: 15m); and employing approximately 15000 people (1994: 60,000) over the next few years.

Uranium

The industry has undergone significant restructuring since 1989 following termination of deliveries to the former Soviet Union and cancellation of purchases by the Slovak Republic. Only three small mines remain in operation and production is likely to be phased out gradually as market conditions do not justify further development or investment.

Uranium requirements are dictated by the fuel requirements of the existing Dukovany nuclear power plants and the new Temelin plants. The government currently purchases the total output and is establishing a strategic stockpile in line with the country's projected needs.

The future

The Czech economy remains highly energy intensive, consuming two to three times the quantity of energy per unit of GDP than in OECD countries. High energy usage results primarily from the continued use by heavy industries of old and inefficient technologies. The privatisation programme is changing this scenario, but slower than is necessary for the country to catch up with western states in the short term. The problems presented by the levels of environmental pollution and above average losses in energy production, conversion, and transport require the application of time as well as massive resources well in excess of the country's capacity.

Nevertheless it is obvious to consultants and others working regularly in the Czech Republic that much is being achieved by way of investment and legislative encouragement to bring the sector up to the government target of OECD comparability. International and bilateral schemes of assistance have been instrumental across a wide range of economic sectors, both domestic and industrial. As an example of these, Cerrex would point to its own involvement in establishing the format for the EU Phare programme's Bank Fund to finance energy saving projects. The key to continued and increased demand for energy efficient equipment and processes remains that of the cost of energy. Once price levels reflect true market conditions the incentive to save energy will be supplied that was so conspicuously absent prior to 1989.

Opportunities for western involvement

The various activities which present opportunities for western involvement basically originate from the Czech Industrial Activity Development Programme established in 1993. These are largely under the control of the Czech Energy Agency within the Ministry of Industry and Trade although other Ministries such as Agriculture and Housing also have significant interests, as do some of the international Agencies such as USAID, EIB (European Investment Bank) and EU. The actual number and scope of the projects together with the other support available for their implementation are too many to be detailed here. For simplicity, however, Cerrex would identify seven principal groupings:

1 energy conservation in industry;
2 energy conservation in transport;
3 energy conservation in agriculture;
4 energy conservation in buildings other than industrial;
5 development of replicable 'cross-sector' techniques;
6 development of utilisation of renewable and secondary energy sources;
7 regional programme of energy conservation.

Many western energy-related equipment manufacturers and consultants have already established a presence in the Czech Republic to meet the rising demand. Considerable scope still exists, however, to introduce new concepts and ideas. As an example Cerrex would cite Energy Performance Contracting/third party finance which is largely undeveloped in the Czech Republic or elsewhere in Eastern Europe, and is seen by us as having a significant future in the region.

14

The Environment

Michael Bird, Cerrex Ltd*

Introduction

Prior to the 'velvet revolution' few resources were allocated to the protection of the environment. The establishment in December 1989 of the Ministry of the Environment concentrated for the first time all jurisdiction in environmental matters which had until then been scattered over various state administrative authorities. The Ministry has primarily been concerned since then with establishing the basis of modern 'environmental' legislation and standards which were completely lacking under the previous regime. Considerable progress has been made and many of the new and proposed measures have been formulated to coincide with European Union requirements. The environmental scene is, however, complicated by a concurrent set of problems resulting from the transformation of the entire economy to a free market basis and the existence of enormous environmental 'debt' incurred in the preceding decades.

Environmental policy

An integral part of the government's reform agenda is the reduction of the environmental impact of industry including energy suppliers and the upgrading of environmental services. This is to be achieved by the application of cleaner technologies, minimisation and appropriate disposal of waste and pollutant discharge, introduction of appropriate legislation and the use of fiscal instruments. These strategic goals can be identified as:

---

*Staff of Cerrex Ltd act as advisors to the Czech government on environment matters.

● **Long-term objectives**   – to make the quality of the environment comparable with the average level of the OECD states in 1990/91 by 2005;

– to make the quality of the environment comparable with the average level of the OECD states by 2015–2020.

Main directions: – minimisation of environmental risks on human health;
– minimisation of activities involving irreversible change to the environment and ecosystems;
– rational use and careful management of non-renewable natural resources;
– gradual integration of environmental issues into all economic and social activities.

● **Medium-Short-term strategy**

Environmental focus:

– waste recycling: cleaner production/ technology;
– water: water protection measures, water/ sewage treatment;
– air: reduction measures (SOx, NOx and solid particulates.

Economic focus:

– energy, industry, transport and agriculture.

The State Environmental Fund (SEF)

One of the major elements of this strategy is the introduction and development of a long-term financial policy to encourage and support environmental projects. Currently this is reflected in the creation of the SEF which is funded primarily from charges for waste water discharge and air pollution emissions and various pollution penalties and fines. The demands on the SEF for assistance, however, greatly exceed (approximately sevenfold) its budget and one area where Cerrex advice has been sought is in the establishment of new funding to be provided under the EU Phare programme. This will be aimed primarily at the industrial sector.

Ongoing programmes

The Ministry of the Environment has established and implemented a number of national and international programmes targeted at the most pressing environmental problems of the Czech Republic. Among these are:

- *An International Commission for Protection of the Labe* was signed with Germany and the EU in October 1990 and has been extended to reduction of the principal sources of pollution throughout the Labe watershed. This covers 65 per cent of the overall Czech territory and involves the construction of a further 30+ water treatment plants.

- *Programme for the Revitalisation of River Systems.* The goal not only aims to increase the ability of the watershed system to retain surface water but also to remedy the negative consequences of land use measures and wide-area drainage (in 1992 35 per cent of agricultural land was excessively drained). Renewal of water courses involves attention to 80,600 km of water courses, of which 5600km are in pipelines and 16,700 km are in artificial canals.

- *Environmental Programme 1.* Carried out in cooperation with the World Bank and a number of European and other states is targeting priority areas. *The Hazardous Waste Handling Centre Project* prepared under the Phare programme is concerned with the construction of suitable technology in Ostravia. *The Communal Services Project* is concerned with providing clean drinking water in the Hradec Kralove-Pardubice Region and the construction of a communal water purification plant in Plzen; with a water management plan for Prague and the handling of communal waste in the Olomouc-Prostejov-Prerov group of cities, and in districts bordering on Bavaria.

- *The Northern Moravia Master Plan* (known as the Silesia project) is a cooperation between the Czech Republic, Poland and the US Environmental Agency on stopping developments detrimental to the environment in the districts of Ostrava, Karvina, Frydek-Mistek, Novy Jicin Bruntal and Opava. Other plans include *The Northern Bohemia Master Plan* (the project for the renewal of lands devastated by mining activities).

- *The National Phare-Environmental Sector programme* funds a wide range of large and small projects. The individual projects cover the protection of human health, protection of water, waste and environmental education. Much of the funding is targeted to the purchase of advanced technology particularly in waste treatment. Phare has also allocated funds for the operation of the Ministry of Environment Banking Environment Fund which is intended to complement the activities of the State Environmental Fund by providing subsidies and 'soft' loans primarily to small and medium-sized businesses.

● *The Black Triangle Programme* is a high priority programme dealing with the severe environmental problems in the Central European coal mining areas in the area between Karlovy Vary and Trutnov, in Saxony and Polish lower Silesia. The EU is financing these activities which are likely to last many years and involve cooperation between Germany, Poland and the Czech Republic.

● *Joint Regional Cooperation Programmes* covering regional environmental problems in Saxony and Bavaria and the protection of water in border areas.

● *Subsidies for environmental projects by Civil Associations in the Czech Republic.* These are especially selected projects connected, for example, with the construction and operation of environmental education centres and environmental consulting and education.

The future

The Czech Republic is determined to become a member of the EU at the earliest possible time. To do so will require meeting many demanding environmental standards currently in force in the EU. The present high emphasis on environmental programmes and the introduction of new technology to clean up the residue of the previous administration is likely to continue for the foreseeable future. The government has also adopted an international stance on the environment and has signed a wide range of international agreements, many of which will continue to provide impetus for the introduction of further domestic legislation. Among these are:

- the convention on Long Range Transboundary air pollution;
- The Vienna Convention on protection of the ozone layer;
- the Basel Convention on control of the transboundary movement of hazardous wastes and their disposal;
- Convention on Transboundary Environmental Impact Assessment;
- Convention on Biological Diversity.

Cerrex's own experience of working in both the energy and environmental sectors indicates a strong and increasing demand for up-to-date environmental technology throughout the Czech economy. The amount of finance available to support this demand is, however, limited and Cerrex would advise interested parties to look to the various aid programmes as a starting point for business in this sector.

15

Utilities

VP International

The key issues with regard to the utilities are privatisation, market pricing and continuity of supply to meet inceasing demand. The Czech nation has been coming to terms with the harsh market realities of adequate payment for public utilities. The days of oversubsidised public services are now long gone. The government has a monumental task on its hands to meet existing and future demand for all public utilities. Estimates for 1995 suggest that anything up to $20 billion will be required to upgrade the entire Czech utility sector.

Privatisation

As in other sectors (such as Banking), the Czech government has not adopted a truly proactive strategy towards unfettered privatisation of utilities. Albeit the transformation of state enterprises has accelerated, as in all the Visegrad countries, it will be a long time before wholesale privatisation is completed in all sectors. The government aimed to complete privatisation of the eight energy (electricity) and eight gas companies by 1995 with the offer of 20 per cent stakes to outside investors, but by the end of 1996 the plan had not been achieved.

Energy policy

Prior to 1990 Czechoslovakia benefited from subsidised Russian energy supplies. The Russians no longer pump unlimited supplies of gas and oil except at what are now realistic market prices. As a consequence, energy costs over the past few years have escalated.

While its energy consumption is very high relative to the country's economic performance, fuel consumption is declining in the Czech Republic as a result of the reconstruction of its primary energy resources.

The Czech government set out the basic principles of its energy policy in 1992, providing guidelines for the constituent parts – technological, economic (industrial), social, ecological and regional. The main features of the policy are:

- regulated privatisation
- conservation
- diversification
- environmental sustainability
- transitional government support
- operational efficiency and reliability
- development of national reserves

The policy is designed to bring the Czech energy sector in line with other EU members as codified in the European Energy Charter. In 1994 an EU report called on the Czech government to phase out all subsidies for gas and electricity and to aid low income families through the social security system (which is slowly but progressively being implemented).

Gas

The key word to gas supply in the Czech Republic is Russia. Supplies of Russian natural gas are scheduled to meet 75–80 per cent of Czech requirements, with the balance to be imported from other countries. Indigenous supplies of natural gas are minimal (approximately 100 million m^3 per annum).

The company responsible for the purchase and supply of natural gas is the state enterprise Transgas, founded in 1971, which handles 7.5 billion m^3 a year.

On 1 January 1994, eight regional joint-stock companies were formed to handle national gas distribution, thus excluding the business of distribution from the state. Up to 34 per cent of the shares are held by local authorities. The Transit Gas Pipeline supplies not only Czech but also other European countries.

Since the distribution reorganisation there has been a significant increase in consumer prices. The government has introduced a new policy (1996) for energy price regulation which has not pleased the distribution companies.

To date the most important international investor has been Gaz de France. British Gas initially showed interest in the market but, tiring of bureaucracy, closed its Prague office in November 1996.

Oil

The 177 km central European oil pipeline, MERO, is the core development project for the country's oil industry. Following the conclusion of lengthy negotiations with the Bavarian authorities for the 30km laid across German territory, supplies commenced to the Czech republic in 1996. Bringing oil via the TAL pipeline from Trieste and through MERO will end the country's dependence on Russian oil. The scheduled MERO capacity is 10 million tonnes of oil a year compared to the seven million agreed with the Russian Federation.

Electricity

The energy giant CEZ is the country's main producer, declaring 1996 year end net profits of CZK 8 billion. Here again there are eight regional privatised companies who, under the new pricing system introduced at the end of 1996, have a 21 per cent share of total sales revenues, with the remaining 79 per cent going to CEZ. In 1997 it is planned to float off 20 per cent stakes in the companies to outside investors. Many European electricity companies have been looking long and hard at the Czech Republic. However, due to Czech governmental prevarication, they have not managed to finalise any investment plans.

Water

Although since 1989 consumption has fallen by 26 per cent, the country still has a relatively high consumption level with 81 per cent of the population consuming over 400 litres per day, compared to an EU average of 300 litres. Water charges have been increased to check consumption.

Principal features of the country's water industry are:

● Many towns still have unacceptably low quality
● Environmental legislation is not being adhered to
● Wastage is still far too high
● National supply is unreliable – 14 per cent of the population are still without tap water
● Sewage pollution is a major problem, resulting in heavily contaminated drinking water. Fifty per cent does not even comply with the country's own environmental standards. It is believed that up to 95 per cent of all well water is contaminated. The Ministry of the Environment launched its 'Rainbow Programme' to tackle this monumental problem inherited from the previous régime.

As with gas, distribution has been transferred to private regional companies. Major reorganisation took place in 1991 whereby ownership was transferred to municipally owned companies. As of 1995 there were 28 joint-stock companies and a further 23 other enterprises managing water supply and sewage treatment. Increasingly state subsidies are being replaced by private capital. French companies predominate, headed by the ubiquitous Compagnie Générale des Eaux. Welsh Water Plc and Gelsenwasser AG have also taken a position in the Czech water industry. It is likely that over the next few years, many more of the municipal water companies will grant concessions to foreign water utilities, in particular the French CGE and LED. However, in spite of an inflow of private capital, there is an acknowledged requirement for continuing government funding for the industry's infrastructure which will last well into the next millennium.

16

Property and Construction

David Lawn, Gleeds

'Look East and prosper' proclaims an article in the *British Building Economist*, which claims that housing output in the Czech Republic is expected to grow by 22.5 per cent a year. The Danish based European Construction Research, a company which prepares reports and seminars on different aspects of the European constuction industry, also predicts uninterrupted growth in the Czech construction sector over the next ten years, with a leap in house construction playing a major role.

It is true that in all the former Communist Central European countries the move to a market-led economy resulted in a massive reduction in house building from which the construction industry has hardly begun to recover. The proportionate value of housing construction remains well below the 25 per cent common in Western European countries, making up only a pitiable 4 per cent of the Czech market. Added to the steady growth in GDP it is easy to see how professional forecasters, armed with statistics, argue convincingly that all the foundations are in place for consistent growth, fuelled by a boom in the housing market.

However there are some major obstacles to be overcome before even the possibility of significant housing growth can be realised in the region. Firstly the inhabitants of post-Communist countries do not enjoy the relatively easy access to mortgage loans common in Western European countries. In the Czech Republic progress has been made, with some state support, but the mechanics remain slow and bureaucratic. Secondly the general lack of infrastructure places huge additional costs on any form of green field development. A further complication is that the utility companies often require developers to obtain all the legal and building permissions for new service lines. This is no easy task in countries where the property restitution process is barely complete, often resulting in numerous new owners who are not inclined to cooperate and who have vastly inflated notions about the value of their inheritance.

This explains why most of the housing developments which have actually made it to the construction phase tend to cater for the top end of the market luxury homes, with huge over demand supporting prices in excess of those in Western Europe. This hardly represents a solution to the problems of a long-term housing shortage which the governments of the region are facing. The policy of simply 'leaving it to the market' will therefore remain a major obstacle to housing growth until it becomes a social issue of substantial political importance. By then the ex-Communists who have found their way back to power may be surprised that the solution has a familiar ring to it – they'll have to sit down and make a plan!

17

The Automotive Industry

VP International

Skoda

Skoda; a Czech national symbol. Czech automotive production and Skoda are synonymous. The Mlada Boleslav-based company dominates virtually all aspects of the country's automotive industry. Skoda is now a totally reformed company, totally different from that which spawned a thousand jokes a few years ago. Now, it has a revitalised product range and image to match. Its products push hard in the small to mid-size range and at prices that are now far from bargain-basement. A quality range of vehicles has emerged from a company that has benefited enormously from the management, stringent quality standards, new component suppliers, design and investment brought by its VW parent. VW's involvement has been very good for Skoda and conversely has also been very good for VW. Skoda is now regarded as one of the jewels in the crown of Volkswagen. What is good for both VW and Skoda has also been good for the country, with increased export earnings (over two-thirds of its vehicles are exported), and a host of international first tier suppliers which have set up shop and have transformed the technologically dated component manufacturing base that characterised the industry pre-1990.

Skoda is the second largest car manufacturer in Central Europe (after Fiat Auto Poland). The company dominates the Czech automotive scene. Save for the production of a few hundred of the lumbering Tatras, Skoda is the Republic's sole volume manufacturer, producing 208,000 cars in 1995 and proposing over 250,000 in 1996. At the start of 1996, one and three-quarter million of all the three million cars on the Republic's roads were Skodas. Fifty-five per cent of new car sales in 1995 were Skodas. Most Czech component companies, plus many of the international firms that have sallied forth into the country, are very heavily dependent on supplying to the firm.

Why VW has not been joined by any other car companies is due to a combination of factors. Primarily this has been due to the limited market size of the country and the attractiveness of setting up in its Polish neighbour which offers a far larger market, lower labour costs and has blatantly dangled far larger carrots in terms of investment incentives and tax breaks to automotive investors.

Sales

Though Skoda dominates domestic market sales (selling 72,078 cars out of the total number of new cars sold in 1995), imported cars are taking an increasing market share. Sales of new imports have doubled over the past two years from 25,324 in 1993 to 56,721 in 1995. A further 119,000 either new personal imports or second hand cars were also brought into the country in 1995.

Figure 17.1 Foreign car sales, 1995 market share (%)

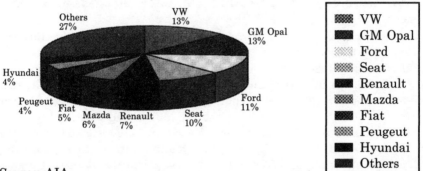

Source: AIA

Though for importers the Czech Republic is not as attractive a market as its northern neighbour Poland, with its 40 million people (ie four times that of the Czech Republic), it still offers a growing potential with rising consumer affluence and an increased demand for newer vehicles. With an average age of car population of over 14 years, and with only 286 cars per thousand at the end of 1995, the country has a long way to go before reaching the ownership levels of its western neighbours.

Components: an international *Who's Who*

Components manufacture has been an entirely different matter. Within five years, the insular industry which served primarily domestic or other Comecon countries has now been transformed into one heavily integrated into international component manufacturing. Whereas prior to 1990, virtually all companies were domestically owned, the picture

today is one where over 50 per cent of all car component companies
are now either owned by, in joint ventures with, or manufactured for,
overseas partners. International component companies present in the
Czech Republic read like a veritable *Who's Who* of the world automotive industry: Ford, VW, Lucas, Packard Electric, Bosch, Ferodo,
Rockwell, Goodyear, Siemens and Continental, to name but a few.

The past few years have most definitely seen a shift eastwards in the
centre of gravity of European component manufacture. With labour
costs (depending on how they are calculated) being one-sixth to
one-tenth of those of Germany, the attraction of Central Europe is
obvious. Even taking into account lower productivity, labour costs per
unit of productivity are considerably lower than those of western
Europe. In particular, its German speaking neighbours have seen many
of its indigenous component companies locate over the former eastern
bloc borders in greater numbers and with greater commitments.

Commercial vehicle production: back on its feet again

Along with all Central European commercial vehicle companies (most
notably those in Hungary), Czech companies saw massive downturns
in the early 1990s. Though now drastically trimmed down from the pre-
1990 era, the industry is just now being turned around with the recent
takeovers of all of the country's major manufacturers. Daewoo's
voracious appetite for the automotive industry in Central Europe was
reflected in its 1995 takeover of Avia by a consortium comprising
Daewoo and Steyr-Daimler-Puch. Daewoo intend this plant to be
a manufacturer of 3.5-7 tonne vehicles, primarily for export markets.
Ambitious plans have been made for Avia, with over 50,000 units
planned for production by the end of the decade (a tenfold increase
from 1995 levels). Over the past year, majority stakeholdings in truck-
makers Tatra and Liaz were acquired by the Skoda automotive
company's heavy engineering namesake, Skoda Plzen. Liaz is now being
put back on the road to recovery after a disastrous early 1990s where
production plummeted from over 20,000 units in 1989 to only 3000 in 1995.
Bus producer Karosa has been put back on its feet with a management
and capital injection from Renault, the EBRD and other Czech partners.

Crystal ball gazing

In terms of a manufacturing sector, the outlook for the Czech automotive
industry must be seen as bright. Though VW now has less ambitious
plans than originally proposed in 1991, Skoda's output will continue to
rise for the rest of the decade and is estimated to peak around 350,000
by the turn of the century. Those international component firms which

have already established themselves will continue to expand their operations. Many of the operations will become significant European production centres, supplying car manufacturers and first tier suppliers across the continent. However, one downside may well be a shortage of labour, which due to the low unemployment rates may well act as a hindrance to attracting further major companies.

As far as car sales are concerned, with growing consumer affluence, the total market for new cars will continue to rise, as will the market share of imported vehicles. Imports will benefit from the progressive removal of tariffs when, at the turn of the century, the Czech Republic will have to conform to common EU duty levels. Needless to say, though its domestic market share will continue to decline, the dominant automotive company in the Czech Republic will inevitably still be...Skoda.

Information sources

If you are a new entrant to the Czech market or are already present and want to be better informed, unfortunately there is no single source of automotive industry information. However, there are a very wide variety of disparate sources whereby adequate market information can be derived. The Czech Automotive Trade Fair in Brno (held each year in May) is the industry forum and is well worth visiting. Furthermore, it is essential to be an exhibitor there if you decide to be a player in this market. The Czech Automotive Industry Association (AIA) is a very cooperative organisation with extensive databases of local companies and well informed staff. The SMMT has an active East European Group which meets quarterly and is a useful forum for swapping information and stories from the front; most UK companies active on the Czech market are members. Many diverse publication sources exist. *Automotive News Europe* and The Economist Automotive Intelligence Unit with its regular *Motor Business International* frequently cover events in Central Europe. The *Financial Times* recently published a report 'Car Manufacturing in Central Europe'. A monthly publication, *Central European Automotive Report* gives a regular appraisal of key industry developments in the region. Finally, VP International offers a press clippings service which scans all the region's English language business press for articles on the automotive industry.

18

Electronics

VP International

Technology gap

For decades Czechoslovakia was cut off from all world development in the electronics industry. The result, when the Czech market opened to the west, was that domestic manufacturers found themselves producing non-competitive products. Prior to 1990 there were state limits on the exchange of information and no permitted interface with the armaments industry which in Russia had received priority funding and scientific know-how. This gap in technology impacted negatively on the economic performance of the new Czech state as it entered a period of industrial and economic reconstruction. From 1989–1992 sales of electrical machinery slumped by 30 per cent. This was due to the country's general economic decline, the exclusion of electrotechnical industries from the first wave of privatisations and its basic lack of consumer appeal, with any existing demand rapidly replaced by cheaper, better quality Asian imports. Today, domestic electronic consumer goods account for just 1 per cent of total electrical engineering production. However, following denationalisation and industry reforms, by the end of 1996 electrotechnical production is expected to rise to 65 per cent of its 1989 level. For the first time for a generation, Czech electrical engineering is producing products that meet market demand.

IT market

The estimated value of the market for hardware plus software in Central Europe (Visegrad countries) is $30 billion and still growing fast. The Western European per capita spend on office automation equipment in 1994 was $100. For the Visegrad countries it was just $23. The market is expected to double by the end of the century.

Initially most of the effort by the major western computer companies (such as Hewlett Packard and IBM) was directed towards satisfying huge government contracts in the tax, finance, social security and land registry administration. The banking industry has been the next largest consumer of IT systems. While the government favoured open systems, the banking sector preference has been for proprietary mainframes. Unisys alone won contracts from the banks for over $200 million. Because of the country's poor telecoms infrastructure and the banks' need for highly centralised systems requiring high security and constantly updated databases, the producers have been able to sell inexpensive   high profit, older tested technologies.

Government IT procurement policy

Any IT companies wishing to supply state organisations, will be governed by the revised legislation and guidelines shown in Table 18.1.

Table 18.1 Issues addressed by legislation and/or guidelines

Ensuring state-funded bodies follow procurement guidelines	Law
Developing as open and fair methods of procurement as possible	Law
Making sure suppliers deliver what they promise	Guideline
Ensuring data on government computers is used for its proper purpose	Law
Developing mechanism to measure IT systems' performance after installation	Guideline
Giving more guidelines to state-funded bodies on what technologies they should favour	No
Fostering an environment in which local firms can successfully compete against foreign suppliers for government contractors	Law

Source : Department of State Information System

Personal computers

The domestic market has become as competitive as any other EU market, with most of the major western brands fighting it out among themselves for a profitable share. Increasingly there are also smaller local producers such as *Libra* now edging into the market, offering competitive prices and good customer after-sales service. This activity has led to a mini price war in the Czech Republic, where VAT at 22 per cent is lower than in Hungary or Slovakia. The inevitable result will be some bankruptcies, particularly among distributors and retailers. Most of the less efficient hardware producers have already gone to the wall.

Choice is extensive and prices are very competitive, so it's good news for consumers of PCs and printers. Major western brands, such as Compaq, IBM and Olivetti all have a strong presence in the marketplace. There is a demand for the very latest specifications. Exposure to western firms has resulted in an increasing transfer of up-to-date technology, with the result that smarter Czech operators are learning to bolt on their own software applications to networked western hardware, and offer a 'turn-key' support service for specific end-users. While price is given as the major incentive for buying, it is important for purchasers to check that warranty, maintenance and other back-up services are all satisfactory. (The standard warranty period is for three years.)

Table 18.2 Market leaders in PC sales – Czech and Slovakia

		Share by volume (%)
Imported PCs	IBM	19
	Compaq	14
Locally made PCs	Vikomt	27
	Escom	12
Printers	Star	29
	Epson	27

Source: BIS strategic division

The main problem is delivery time as the leading brands don't hold big stocks in Central Europe, preferring to fulfil orders out of established EU distribution centres.

Software

Perhaps the biggest IT challenge has been the cost and time required for the translation of western software packages. This an area where local companies have successfully stepped in. For example the Czech company Software602 captured most of the domestic MS-DOS word-processing market with its Text602 package, outselling all foreign competitors between 1989–93. Another local success story is the APP Group a.s. with annual sales of $35 million. The western majors have taken an investment strategy in the marketplace, understanding that software sales are cumulative. Microsoft even donated $7 million worth of programmes to the Ministry of Education. Prices are low and competitive.

The leading company in the expanding financial software market is the German group SAP which is being challenged strongly by the California-based Oracle Corporation. Other players include the US giant SunSystems and Sweden's Beslutsmodeller.

As might be expected, piracy is endemic with an estimated 80 per cent of all software in the Czech Republic being copied illegally.

Legislation is in place with custodial penalties for the guilty and the Business Software Alliance has been formed to 'police' the market. However it seems that in practice there have been few prosecutions.

Fax and photocopiers

Unlike the market for PCs and printers, sales of fax and photocopiers will probably fall over the course of the next few years, largely because there will be a much slower rate of replacement and upgrade.

Table 18.3 Market leaders – fax and photocopiers

		Estimated market share 1996 (%)
Photocopiers	Canon	22
	Minolta	20
Fax machines	Panasonic	42
	Canon	23

Source: BIS strategic division

Televisions

Consumer electronics was never a successful industrial feature of the old communist Central European bloc. What producers there were have all but disappeared as the 'Asian invasion' takes an ever-increasing hold on the market. In January 1996 Matsushita announced it would invest $66 million in a greenfield manufacturing site to produce 1 million Panasonic TV sets a year by 1997. Simultaneously, the declining fortunes of the old Czechoslovakia's only TV manufacturer, OTF, are typical; they now hold less than 20 per cent of the domestic market.

19

Industry

Cerrex Ltd

Level of investment in the Czech Republic

Investment in the Czech Republic offers investors considerable advantages, wage rates averaging only a quarter of EU levels, a highly educated and skilled workforce and access to markets not traditional to UK exporters. Between 1990 and March 1996, total foreign investment in the Czech Republic was estimated at $US 6 billion. Germany (approximately $1.8 billion) with its close historical and geographical connections dominates with the USA, Switzerland and Netherlands (each about $850 million); France ($550 million); Austria ($300 million, Italy, Belgium and Denmark make up the top nine investors.

Level of UK investment

UK investment was just under CZK 3 billion (US$108 million) or 1.8per cent of the total and about half the amount invested by the Belgians and somewhat less than the Danes. The UK is outside the top nine investors.

Table 19.1 Levels of UK investment

Sector	1990 to 31 March 1996 CZK(m)	%
Trade and services	558.3	18.8
Chemical industry	448.4	15.1
Food industry	855.4	28.8
Electronics	316.4	10.7
Others	790.7	26.6
Total	2968.9	100.0

Source: Czech Statistic Office

Table 19.2 Major UK investments in the Czech Republic

Foreign Partner	Type of Business	Commitment (CZK)	Time Span	Name of Czech Partner
Bass Breweries	Beer	2.7bn	1993–1998 Oct 1995	Prazske pivovary–39 per cent US$ 32m. 1993 Vratislavice– 55% & Ostrava 34 % for US$ 22m. Oct 1995
Shell Czech Republic	Gas	445m	1992–1994	Shell's operation in the Czech Republic is independent of local companies
Tesco	Retailing	1.8bn	March 1996	Maj dept. store
Metzeler	Auto parts	60m	1994	Metzeler, s.r.o
AVX/Kyocera	Electronics	874m	1993	AVX Ceska republika Kyocera Group
Welsh Water	Waste water treatment	310m	1995	Severoceske vodovody a kan alizace–35% stake
Lucas	Autoparts			Ateso, a.s. Jablonec n. Nisou

Source: Czech Statistic Office

Light industry

Textile, clothing and leather industries have remained fifth in the country by production, and third by employment and export share. Some 50 per cent of product is exported. These figures conceal a halving of overall production since 1990 (the big drop came in 1991), and the need to improve the quality of the products and move towards the fashion market. Privatisation has not led to as much inward investment as had been anticipated, and western firms have generally expressed a preference for jobbing contracts rather than joint ventures.

Table 19.3 Light industry 1993–1996

	1993	1994	1995	1996 (Estimate)
Total production [1, 2] (Bn CZK)	33.2	33.5	33.7	33.8
Total number of employees (thousands)	196	190	182	169
Total domestic market (Bn CZK)	46.9	48.6	58.1	65

Source: Czech Statistic Office

1 Based on CSO figures for firms employing 25 or more people, adjusted by number of employees and known production ratios

2 At constant prices 1989 *Source:* CSO and Cerrex Ltd estimates for 1996

Textiles

1995 saw a growth of 8.7 per cent in textiles and 3.7 per cent in clothing. New domestic retail shops are emerging but competition from western firms such as Benetton and Kleider Bauer makes domestic sales by Czech companies more difficult and has forced the industry to change product mix away from standard products to better design and quality. It is still uncertain where the capital will come from to replace production machinery as financial returns of companies in bulk textiles (and leather) have declined. There is mounting pressure from the industry for controls on imports and action to provide export incentives. Duties on Czech textiles exports into the EU are being steadily reduced and the import quotas are due to cease on Czech textile exports to the EU during 1997. At the beginning of 1996, there were an estimated 481 companies in the textile sector of which over 60 per cent had fewer than 200 employees, and there are considerable investment opportunities presented by the expected rationalisation of the industry.

Footwear and leather goods

The Czech footwear industry is reorganised around the SG group at Zlin, which holds stakes in some 13 companies, employing about 7000 people and exporting about 45 per cent of output. Production of footwear fell from about 50 million in 1990 to 30 million in 1995, mainly because of loss of traditional markets in USSR and cheap Far Eastern imports. The need to reorganise production units and marketing has been delayed by the shortage of capital, but Svit has made up some lost ground by increasing exports to the European Union through agreements with Danish, German and Austrian companies.

Tanning and leather

Most of the tanneries (some 15) based in Zlin and Jaromer (the centre for light leather) have been privatised and a number of plants run by Tanex closed. The presence of inexpensive and highly skilled labour has not prevented a considerable decline in output and low capacity utilisation mainly because of the shortage of raw hides, loss of part of the domestic end user market to Far Eastern imports, and the cost of meeting environmental controls. Disposal of waste such as chrome and the control of water pollution are the major problems facing the sector, and could have a considerable effect on its future.

Paper, board, wood, pulp, furniture, and associated industries

Since 1993 the paper, printing and pulp industries have fared better than primary timber and furniture and benefited from substantial investment. The previously less developed markets for newspapers, magazines and advertising, and exports, have received a new impetus and there has been an explosion in the number of private print shops fitted with new, high quality equipment. There has been increasing competition from imports in the Czech market for coated paper, hygiene products, furniture, printed and wooden products including toys, sporting goods, health care articles, brushes, and for products for the treatment and processing of timber, and the expanding market for these products has stimulated investment for modernisation.

Table 19.4 Wood, pulp, paper, printing and publishing industries

	1993	1994	1995	1996 (estimate)
Total production [1,2] (Bn CZK)	40.1	42.1	45.4	47.0
Total number of employees (thousands)	161	157	151	140
Total domestic demand (Bn CZK)	63.5	71.8	80.5	100

Source: Czech Statistic Office

1 Based on CSO figures for firms employing 25 or more people, adjusted by number of employees and known production ratios

2 At constant prices 1989 *Source:* CSO and Cerrex Ltd estimates for 1996

Heavy investment in paper and pulp has been encouraged in the belief that demand for paper will treble over the next ten years, that paper prices would continue to increase until at least 1998 and raw material costs were unlikely to increase by more than 10 per cent during the same period. EBRD has made available several lines of credit for use in the modernisation of production and improved quality so that it can compete with international pulp firms. New markets are opening up for firms awarded ISO9001 quality assurance. There has been increasing production of recycled paper, although this slowed down with the general fall in demand for paper at the end of 1995.

The sector is continuing to look for strategic partners offering training and marketing skills and to help firms integrate into the European market – links with the EU producer Assidoman have given Biocel Paskov and SEPAP, for example, access to European sales and distribution networks, and allowed them to restructure and develop joint ventures with Austrian and Slovak companies and concentrate on areas where they are most competitive, eg the bleached pulp and packaging markets.

Glass, ceramics and building material

The reputation of the glass and ceramics trade has remained very high worldwide with a strong and profitable export base. Interest from foreign overseas investors has been strong Glaverbel took over the main flat glass manufacturer Glave Union Teplice, while St Gobain, Vetropack and Laufen have also become involved. Domestic and foreign investment has also gone into machinery for the production of new lines for industrial glass, modernisation of decorative glass manufacture, cement, sanitary ceramics and the production of floor and wall tiles, bricks and roofing materials (see Table 19.5).

Table 19.5 Glass, ceramics and building materials industry

	1993	1994	1995	1996 (estimate)
Total production (Bn CZK) [1, 2]	18.4	19.3	20.0	22.5
Total number of employees (thousands)	76	73	64	61
Total domestic Market (Bn CZK)	23.4	26.8	32.7	35

Source: Czech Statistic Office

1 Based on CSO figures for firms employing 25 or more people, adjusted by number of employees and known production ratios

2 At constant prices 1989 *Source:* CSO and Cerrex Ltd estimates for 1996

Decorative cut glass

This is one of the two sectors (beer is the other) where there is national feeling against foreign involvement. The reputation and profit margins of some firms is sufficient for them not to require foreign investment, although they still welcome strategic alliances. Many of the most famous are in private hands, eg Sklarny Bohemia, Sklo Bohemia and Jihlavske Sklarny Bohemia. Investment programmes since 1991 have concentrated on improvement in quality.

The sector has maintained its position of distributing directly. Some of the Czech companies have chosen to specialise. The country is a major exporter of jewellery, with about 20 per cent of the world market, and a 35 per cent share of glass beads produced by Zasada. Preciosa is one of the world's largest producers of machine cut glass stones, and it has successfully established its own export network reorienting its markets to western Europe and the Far East.

Technical and laboratory glass

Technical and laboratory glass are the most progressive branches of the glass industry, especially in the areas of traditional laboratory glass, test tubes and thermometers, household flame-proof glass, so that today some two-thirds of total glass production in the country is in the industrial sector. Sklarny Kavalier Sazava, for example, former producers of pharmaceutical and lighting glass, now produce heat resistant household glass under the SIMAX mark, technical and laboratory glass. Those Czech companies which meet ISO 9002 rating are targeting microwave manufacturers, pharmaceutical companies and auto-glass.

Building Materials

Initially the sector did not live up to the expectations that specialists had predicted due primarily to the changes in methods of building after 1990 which led to a reduction in domestic consumption of cement, and the decline in road building. The situation has changed considerably since 1993 with rapid increases in production of cement and lime and investors are optimistic about the long term – German interests have taken a controlling interest in one of the three major wall tile companies (Rackoniche). Austrian investment has gone into roof tile manufacture and three of the ten largest foreign investments in the country have gone into the cement industry. New production methods have been introduced – for example high burn technology for roof tiling. The future depends very much on the local construction industry which is projected to grow 7–8 per cent per year to 2000, and supplying neighbouring markets. As a country with enormous kaolin reserves, opportunities also lie in the development of kaolin as an improving agent in the pipe industry and advanced electronics with electromagnetic applications.

Chemicals and pharmaceuticals

Conventional wisdom argues that the best opportunities in the sector are in pharmaceuticals, speciality chemicals, processing of crude polyamide, niche sectors such as production of components for drugs, paints, agrochemicals and flavourings. Increased production in these sectors has not outweighed the decline in other sectors such as oil processing and bulk chemicals. The industry's own investment plans include expansion of organic dyestuffs, speciality synthetic resins, pure chemicals and modern industrial agents. The 1996 Czech state budget earmarked $12 million for environmentally friendly projects in the sector. The construction of the present Ingolstadt pipeline, to be completed by the end of the decade, should help cooperation between the western petrochemical industry and the Czech organic chemistry industry. Chemicals are expected to become a priority sector for activity by CzechInvest after 1996 concentrating on petrochemicals and plastics for the electronics and automotive sectors.

Table 19.6 Chemicals and pharmaceuticals

	1993	1994	1995	1996 (estimate)
Total production [1,2] (Bn CZK)	51.7	54.8	57.8	69.3
Total number of employees(thousands)	92	89	83	83
Total domestic market (Bn CZK)	131.5	143.0	173.7	n.a.

Source: Czech Statistic Office

1 Based on CSO figures for firms employing 25 or more people, adjusted by number of employees and known production ratios

2 At constant prices 1989 *Source* CSO and Cerrex Ltd estimates for 1996

Little substantial modernisation has taken place in the chemical sector – although the sector is well endowed with know-how production and exports tend to be in the area of bulk tonnages, with a relatively low degree of processing and is in need of technology and investment.

The balance of trade has become increasingly negative, with imports consisting primarily of sophisticated products. Although the demand for bulk chemicals might increase – perhaps in line with Czech national demand for petrol and increased motorisation over the next 10–15 years – it is very uncertain whether margins will increase. The Chemapol oil and chemical company is expanding, looking to partners in Romania and for worldwide cooperation in the pharmaceutical industry, and the Taipei Board of Commerce has said that companies from Taiwan hope to establish three industrial estates in the Republic over two years – with up to 40 Taiwanese chemical companies involved.

Pharmaceuticals is already an area of substantial UK involvement (including Glaxo, SKB, Zeneca and Sterling), and more investment is required to increase the share of more sophisticated products in total output. The Czech pharmaceutical industry is generally considered to be self-financing, more in need of expertise and markets than in foreign capital, although Czech firms will need to spend extensively to maintain their strong R and D position in this area. Competition from well-established global competitors in Germany and Switzerland will substantially influence their potential for growth.

Mining

A rapid decline in demand from the former COMECON and from the major Czech steel manufacturing companies, improved energy efficiency, reduction of coal subsidies, rise of nuclear power alternatives and the use of more modern production techniques making better use of raw materials have affected mineral extraction over the past two years. The country has mined progressively decreasing amounts of hard and brown coal – although exports have trebled over the past five years – and is expected to contract further. Other products mined include iron, lead, zinc, uranium, gold, lime and kaolin.

Exploitation of some small sites can be expected for non-ferrous metals including uranium, but generally no growth is expected. The future of gold mining, in the Sumava mountains and at Mokrske in central Bohemia, which at one time appeared to be in the balance, has received considerable publicity. The original survey estimated that mines at Mokrske would last 15–20 years and bring in up to $25 billion in taxes. Concern over the environment, however, methods of mining and their possible effect on the water supply has led to a slow-down in investment and there has been political opposition to allowing foreign investors to have access to rare metals.

Metallurgy

Under the CMEA, the Czech Republic produced considerable volumes of steel, but investment was intermittent, and production took place on a mixture of modern and outdated equipment (in 1990 only about 14 per cent was produced on the electric process and continuous castings less than 10 per cent), although total efficiency was relatively high because of low energy prices. The Czech industry appears the least outdated of all Eastern European metallurgy industries, and its future will depend very much on the revival in demand from its main domestic engineering and construction customers. Some rationalisation would be expected as and when the Republic joins the EU. The sector has found difficulty in balancing the loss of former USSR markets with increased exports to the EU.

Table 19.7 Metallurgy and metalworking

	1993	1994	1995	1996
Total production [1,2] (Bn CZK)	66.7	69.5	82.3	85
Total number of employees (thousands)	227	212	220	185
Total domestic market (Bn CZK)	99.6	115.1	166.2	200

Source: Czech Statistic Office

1 Based on CSO figures for firms employing 25 or more people, adjusted by number of employees and known production ratios

2 At constant prices 1989 *Source*; CSO and Cerrex Ltd estimates for 1996

A main question mark is whether the Czech economy is large enough to support three large steelmakers. With recent steps towards privatisation, Nova Hut, Vitkovice and Trinecke Zelezany have started costly development programmes including retooling of plants, modernising production with the introduction of new mini mills, continuous casting processes and reduction of energy costs, improvement of quality standards and all are looking for particular niches into which they can consolidate. The main firms also require restructuring – Vitkovice, for example, traditionally also undertook a 'social role' running hotels, hospitals, schools, shops, and they are expected to be split into smaller manageable parts and to spin off their engineering subsidiaries into downstream operations. Joint ventures in such areas are expected to be more interesting to western interests. Diversification of engineering products has included production of metal wheels for cars and new clients include BMW, Mercedes, Audi, Opel and Fiat.

Plans drawn up in the early 1990s foresaw the need to restructure the Czech (and Slovak) steel industry, envisaging a fall in production by some 27 per cent between 1991–2000 and reducing the number employed by two thirds.

Engineering (excluding automotive)

The Czech Republic has reputedly one of the widest variety of engineering products of any country and Western European firms have found that sourcing components, licensing and cooperation agreements, complementing their product range, have presented better opportunities than direct sales. In 1995 manufacture of machinery and equipment equalled 9 per cent of total manufacturing production, 16 per cent of employment and 11.7 per cent of total exports. 1995 and 1996 saw steady increases in output and expectations are that growth will take place in roughly one–third of the general engineering sector. Imports, however, are taking an increasing share of the market, even against entrenched domestic suppliers. The need to meet environmental standards, the rising cost of energy and the world market situation are encouraging a continuing move from heavy engineering.

Table 19.8 Engineering

	1993	1994	1995	1996 (estimate)
Total production [1, 2] (Bn CZK)	32.8	31.4	33.6	37
Total number of employees (thousands)	218	198	184	162
Total domestic demand (Bn CZK)	92.6	99.6	120.5	145

Source: Czech Statistic Office

1 Based on CSO figures for firms employing 25 or more people, adjusted by number of employees and known production ratios

2 At constant prices 1989 *Source:* CSO and Cerrex Ltd estimates for 1996

The three major heavy engineering firms (CKD Prague, Skoda Plzen and PBS) have bought back some of their previous operations, taken over plants overseas, eg Skoda Plzen has bought a facility in Germany, and in some cases extended the operation, ie Skoda Plzen have bought Tatras and Liaz (truck manufacturers at Liberec). All have stayed in Czech hands, although they have set up joint ventures with foreign operators and all three appear to be profitable. Many other firms have privatised using foreign investment – ABB have a strong presence with 10–12 production companies and VW investment in Skoda (motor cars) is probably the most well known. Sterling Tools have taken advantage of low labour costs to hold down production cost against competition from Far Eastern suppliers in the EU market.

Many local Czech engineering companies have modern equipment, and those which have managed to reorganise and introduce efficient marketing, changing the psychological environment to a more commercial one, are generally profitable. Finance has become less of a problem – interest rates have been falling and with a good business plan and a trade record companies are now more likely to obtain credit from banks. Main problems they have to face are meeting new environmental standards, upgrading working practices, and opening up new markets to compliment former major markets in the ex-Soviet Union, Vietnam, Korea, North Africa and a number of Arab countries. These companies provide opportunities for UK joint venture firms to enter non-traditional markets.

It is not possible to be precise as to where best prospects lie for UK industry. There are obvious advantages to western companies. Renault's take over of Karosa, for example, allowed it to gear production from the Czech plant towards developing country markets, and for Renault to reduce substantially its price to Western Europe and developed markets, using cheaper skilled Czech labour, while improving quality and financial return in Karosa.

Table 19.9 Wage comparison: US$ annual: total average remuneration 1995*

	Czech Rep	Hungary	Poland
Plant manager	16,621	32,913	30,056
Head of Human Resources	14,064	24,380	19,859
Production manager	10,839	15,472	13,519
Secretary	6,286	12,659	11,626
Warehouse supervisor	5,893	7,400	9,381
Buyer	4,795	5,532	5,230
Electrician	4,201	4,464	6,330
Skilled operator	3,649	4,185	4,850

Source: CzechInvest

*Total remuneration includes salary and wages, bonuses, profit sharing, cost of living and local market value adjustments. Add-ons range from approximately 36 – 55 per cent. Wage inflation is 10–15 per cent per annum (compared to general inflation of about 9.6 per cent).

Major growth areas for 1996 and beyond will be in the energy/heat savings sector, transport machinery, the purchase of components for complete industrial plants, electrical and optical equipment, glass manufacturing machinery, printing and textile machinery, waste water treatment equipment, pumps and industrial cleaning equipment, turbines, compressors, furnaces and machine tools, construction machines; and the development of turbines and compressors presents opportunities for collaboration.

Precision engineering is one of the three main areas (including electronics and automotive) where Czechinvest is making a special effort to encourage investment. The sector is noted for its skilled engineering, micro assembly, plastic moulding skills and technology (with sub-assembly press work of sintering, die casting also major sectors of the industry) aimed primarily at the automotive, capital goods and electronics sectors making to ISO 9000 standard. The sector is undertaking an increasing amount of outsourcing and sub-assembly work for western manufacturing companies. The country has a very high percentage of degrees awarded in science and engineering, and Prague CVVT is the largest of European technical universities with around 15,000 students. The competitive costs base is one of the main advantages of the Czech industry compared to its neighbours. Firms that have taken advantage include Mannesman; Siemens; Rockwell; Ford; TRW; Lucas; VW; GM; Ferrodo; Daewoo; Allied Signal; Honeywell.

The country's practical technology base is weak and the supply of technology from Western Europe will be required in both the service and industrial sectors. For example, in the banking sector, Kommercni Banka has installed Microsoft Windows 95 throughout the group; SPT, the state telecom operator, has started a multibillion dollar programme up to 2000. The requirement for GSM mobile telephone services is likely to lead to significant imports of transmission equipment. The construction of the pipeline from Ingolstadt in Germany to Czech refineries and the modernisation of Skoda autos as started in 1991 (and latterly for other parts of the automotive sector) is revitalising the component industry. Refineries are also about to undertake a long modernisation programme following the investment agreement with western oil companies.

A substantial element of the proposed modernisation includes environmental improvement. Sales of environmental technology are likely to increase especially to firms in heavy engineering, steel and energy. New laws on environmental standards are due to come into force in 1997, forcing changes/investment in processes on industries, and firms have gone or will go out of business. CEZ, the electrical utility, is engaged in a costly clean-up of its coal-burning power stations to meet the conditions of the new regulations, and is spending heavily on imported technology. There are pressures from certain sectors of Czech industry for the government to give financial encouragement to develop an environmental engineering industry. Many companies are diversifying into the production of environmental equipment but may require to source the technology under licensing agreements and joint ventures.

20

Telecommunications

Ivan Sloboda, CEE Telecom Projects

Historical background and the present set-up

The former Czechoslovakia was one of the more economically developed countries in the pre-1989 Communist bloc. Within this bloc Czechoslovakia's telecommunications facilities were one of the most developed, although they were well below Western European standards. Without a market economy this state-owned monopoly operator, subject to COCOM restrictions, suffered from underinvestment into what was regarded as a non-priority sector and lacking suitable regulation. In the wake of 1989 changes, the Czechoslovak telecommunication inheritance was similar to that of its Eastern neighbours, ie obsolete analogue networks, long waiting lists, poor quality of service and low telephone penetration.

The telecommunications network is a large, complex and investment-intensive system with a life cycle often as long as 50 years. Even to the optimists it was clear that the changes would take many years and require massive funding. The greatest problem remains the local telecommunications network, which is always the most expensive part of the infrastructure and which takes many years to install.

Historically equipment has been manufactured locally or within the Eastern bloc; although usable, much of the equipment became obsolete virtually overnight. Modern equipment available from the West is pegged to western prices, while the telecommunications revenue needed to finance the modernisation has been low due to tariff limitations. These were, and remain, rigorously applied by the Czech government to control inflation.

After the division of Czechoslovakia and the establishment of the Czech Republic (January 1993), the Ministry of Economy assumed responsibility for telecommunications activities in the Czech Republic. The state administration sections were supplemented with a regulatory section which together comprise the Czech Telecommunications Office, very recently moved into the Ministry of Transport and Communications.

At the same time the Administration of PTT, ie the operator known as SPT Praha, was split into the two new state enterprises. One was the postal operator, the other SPT Telecom – *de facto* a telecommunications state-owned operator. In parallel these developments were augmented by a Telecommunications Law opening up possibilities for liberalisation, privatisation and competition, as well as the separation of regulatory and operational functions. The responsibility for the all-important inland telecommunications tariff was allocated to the new Czech Finance Ministry.

SPT Telecom became a state-owned joint stock company in January 1994. In the second wave of privatisation, which started at the same time, SPT Telecom was privatised.

The tender process for a foreign partner was completed in June 1996 and Telsource, a consortium of PTT Telecom Netherlands (51 per cent) and Swiss PTT (49 per cent) with the non-equity participation of AT and T, was selected. This completed the last step in the privatisation process: the sale took the form of a 34 per cent increase in the share capital of SPT Telecom, equivalent to a 27 per cent stake in the overall company, which was purchased for around US $ 1.45 billion.

The telecommunications networks

SPT Telecom is primarily responsible for the operation of the switched voice network. The end-of-1995 figures indicate some 2.4 million direct exchange lines, a telephone density of 23.3 per 100 population (42.2 per cent of households with telephones), and a waiting list of some 657 thousand potential customers. Some 50 000 km of fibre optic cable was installed by the end of that year. The monopoly of SPT Telecom was dented in 1995 when the government issued 16 licences to operate local telecommunications networks, mainly to the existing CATV operators who were keen to enter the telephony market. Private voice networks are also operated by the Czech Railways (CD) and the Czech Power Supply Utility (CEZ). In the area of wireless local access networks, SPT Telecom is conducting pilot projects using fixed cellular radio networks in the south-western part of Prague, the DECT system in Brno and a rural system in South Bohemia.

The analogue public cellular system is provided by Eurotel Praha Ltd, a joint venture between SPT Telecom and US West/Bell Atlantic using NMT 450 technology. More recently two GSM licences have been issued: one to the existing analogue operator Eurotel Praha Ltd, with the other to Radiomobil, a joint venture between Czech Radiocommunications and the foreign-owned T-Mobil (major shareholder DeTe Mobil). Both GSM Systems are now in use.

Nextel o.z., wholly owned by SPT Telecom, is the sole data network operator providing mainly X.25, X.75 and X.400 services. The public paging service is provided by Radiocontact Operator Prague – a joint venture between Czech Radiocommunications and France Telecom.

Czech Radiocommunications, part-owned by the Government and by private investors, provides broadcasting and radiocommunication networks. There are several companies providing Internet, VSAT and entertainment CATV services.

Type approval

The Czech Telecommunication Office, Department of Certification, is responsible for type approval of telecommunication equipment. It works closely with Testcom, an accredited telecommunication laboratory.

British presence and future opportunities

In the early stages of the post–1989 development the most visible UK presence was through British consultants and advisors, such as BT Telconsult and PA Consulting Group, financed by various aid agencies/banks. The main players in the Czech sector are aware of the British strengths in this field, closely connected with the privatisation and liberalisation processes in the UK.

More recently the Motorola manufacturing facility at Swindon has won a major infrastructure equipment supply contract from the RADIOMOBIL GSM network. Similarly GPT won a large contract for the provision of transmission (SDH) equipment to SPT Telecoms. BT has extended its CONCERT network into the Czech Republic with its local partner GTS.

The market is becoming progressively more westernised and competitive, with a favourable credit rating, a strong presence of western suppliers and financially strong operators. Massive contracts for public switching equipment will not be available for a number of years (Alcatel and Siemens currently share this market). Similarly, due to GPT's recent success, similar contracts for transmission equipment will also not be available for the next two to three years. However, the market offers opportunities in VSAT, microwave equipment for frequencies above 23 GHz, Global Positioning Equipment, metallic and fibre cables (private network operators, but not SPT), terminal equipment, data communications equipment (Nextel and the Czech Railways), Internet systems and general test equipment. Traditionally British consultants, experienced in competitive environments, enjoy a good reputation in the Czech Republic although this area is extremely competitive. There is also considerable potential for niche equipment serving specialised local needs such as equipment for quickly upgrading/increasing the capacity of local networks.

There is no readily available network of distributors and whole-salers. Therefore, a potential exporter needs to rely on local knowledge such as is provided by local agents or by the commercial section of the British Embassy in the form of a Market Information Report. These may be requested via the Department of Industry's local offices in the UK. Any exporter needs to be aware of the purchasing influence exer-cised by western partners in the major operator joint ventures. Potential investors should examine a number of opportunities in future operating companies as the competitive environment is very much encouraged by the present Government. Investors also need to be aware of opportunities in new services such as Internet access, where often a local company, with good expertise, is unable to raise the necessary funds alone. Potential returns appear to be attractive.

21

Media

VP International

Since the dismantling of the state monopolies, the Czech media market has developed into one of the region's most sophisticated. All forms of media have burgeoned over the past five years. State control of every aspect of the media has largely been replaced by innumerable private and, in many cases, international groups. Advertising in all its genres has consequently boomed with expenditure reaching CZK 11 billion in 1996, which represents approximately 1 per cent of GDP.

Table 21.1 Advertising Expenditure (1995)

Press	46
TV	36
Outdoor	9
Radio	6
Other	2

Source : IP Praha

Print

Print media have made the most rapid free-market transition with western capital flowing in to fill the vacuum left by the state's withdrawal. Western media groups (in particular German ones) have bought national titles or have launched numerous Czech language variations of western titles.

There are 160 main periodicals; the principal titles are represented in Table 21.2 (over).

Table 21.2 Principal Periodicals

Title	Publisher	Readership (%)
Mlada fronta dnes	Rheinisch Bergischen	14
Blesk (tabloid)	Ringier	13
Pravo		10
ZN noviny	Mitteirhein Verlag Bohemia	6
Svobodne Slovo		4
Hospodarske Noviny	Handelsblatt	3
Prace		3
Sport		3
Expres	Mitteirhein Verlag Bohemia	3
Lidove noviny	Ringier	3

Source: Czech Media & Marketing

Broadcast media

After the velvet revolution, pluralist broadcasting became a priority and a dual state/private system has emerged. The industry is organised along the following lines:

- State TV
  CT1 – cultural programmes prioritised – viewership 20 per cent
  CT2 – channel for particular viewers – viewership 3 per cent

- Commercial TV
  TV Nova – viewership 71 per cent
  Launched in 1994 by Vladimir Zelezny, TV Nova was the first national commercial television station in the former communist bloc. With an audience share of over 70 per cent it claims the highest market share of any national terrestrial TV station in Europe. In 1996 the American media group CME (Central European Media Enterprises Ltd) acquired Ceska Sporitelna Bank's 22 per cent share for CZK 1 billion.

- *Premiera TV* – viewership 2 per cent
  A small regional station.

Commercials can run during all TV programmes, except news, religious and children's. Tobacco advertising is regulated and is not permitted on radio between 6 a.m. and 10 p.m.

Research

Press and radio media are relatively well researched via Media Projekt, with a database representing 99 per cent of all Czech households. Fifteen thousand interviews are conducted annually and updated four times a year. The reports are produced jointly by GfK Praha and Median.

Shortly to be installed in 600 households is an *AGB 4900 Peoplemeter*. However, the advertising agencies and the TV companies are in dispute over the measured unit of viewing time. Nova TV wants data in 15-minute increments while the ad. agencies are demanding more accurate minute-by-minute results for their clients. It is likely that the advertisers will win the day, necessitating the agencies having to fund at least 10 per cent of the investment costs (some CZK 60 million over the next five years). Additionally, the agencies will have to pay the provider, Taylor Nelson AGB, CZK 1 million p.a. software rental fee plus CZK 500 000 per annum, for the data itself. Already they have to pay Media Projekt for print and radio research data.

Cable TV

When originally set up in the early 1990s the industry used out-of-date loop line serial wiring because it was cheap and easy to install. This has led to expensive rebuilding of the initial connections with the star configuration. The key to winning audiences is programming in the Czech language, but this requires major funding and a longer payback than in the West. Hence there has been a heavy reliance on imported material.

- By far the largest operator is **Cable Plus**, with 420 000 viewers in the Czech Republic and Slovakia and a market share of 0.5 per cent. Founded by Petr Siroky, a 28 per cent stake was acquired in May 1995 by US West International for $19 million. But due to some 40 per cent of the company's 'customers' defaulting on subscription payments (the outdated technology did not permit them to cut off non-payers), US West has increased its investment to $90 million by way of loans and an increased equity stake.

- **Kabel Net**, founded in 1993 and owned by Denver-based United International Holdings (the largest cable operator in Europe), claims 30,000 customers.

- **Dattel** has approximately 15 000 customers in the Prague area.

- There is a fourth cable company, **Codis**, but its customer base is not published.

Digital

January 1997 will see the launch of **CzechLink**, a digital broadcasting joint venture between Premiera TV, Kabel Plus and state-owned Czech Television. It represents the first move into digital broadcasting in Central and Eastern Europe. The technology has been purchased from Philips at a cost of CZK 50 million. Once installed, programmes will be broadcast to homes and local cable operators via Deutsche Telekom's Kopernikus satellite using the MPEG2 compression system.

The digital satellite system will replace the current terrestrial system at Czech TV, so improving the coverage of CTV's second channel, CT2. It will also reduce the companies' dependency on the state monopoly *Ceske radiokomuniocace*, broadcaster of TV and radio signals.

Radio

The principal stations are shown in Table 21.3.

Table 21.3 *Principle radio stations*

Station	Ownership	Listenership (%)
Frekvence 1	*commercial*	16
Czech Radio 1-Radiozurnal	*state*	15
Czech Radio 2-Praha	*state*	11
Radio Nova Alfa	*commercial*	6
Europa 2 National	*commercial*	3
Czech Radio 3-Vltava	*state*	1

Source : Czech Media & Marketing

Advertising

All major international agencies have established full service agencies. Their stated aim is to employ western experience and technology to develop local creativity and not simply to produce a clone of the US industry, which is how things started out.

However, in spite of the presence of all the big names, the market should still be regarded as in its infancy, though it is steadily progressing towards the levels of sophistication as seen in most western countries. The Association of Advertising Agencies of the Czech Republic (ARA) with 70 advertising and media members, represents the industry and is a member of the European Association of Advertising Agencies (EAAA).

Public relations

PR is still a fledgling industry but, again, some of the principal world players have offices in Prague. They are represented by the APRA – the Association of Czech PR Agencies – and their members include:

- Amalthea
- Ogilvy & Mather Focus
- Hill & Knowlton
- Burson-Marsteller
- Interel
- Elisa – EMC Group
- Pragma and Motoska PR+Consulting.

22

Health Care Changes

VP International

Massive changes in all aspects of the organisation of health care provision are being seen throughout Central Europe. The interminable debates and complaints about health care provision in the UK (namely underfunding of the NHS, standards of care, creeping privatisation and so on) are being raised, no less vigorously across Central Europe and no more so than in the Czech Republic. Most observers would agree that the health care system in the Czech Republic has fundamental problems, not least of which are the issues regarding private versus public funding and escalating costs.

From an outsider's point of view, on the positive side for western manufacturers, the opening up of this formerly closed Central European market has presented new opportunities for overseas medical suppliers to sell into a market which is expanding rapidly.

Health care reforms

Since the collapse of communism in 1989, there have been progressive reforms in the health care system of the Czech Republic. This has culminated in a health care system run increasingly on a commercial basis, and based on an obligatory insurance scheme, as opposed to a centrally controlled and run national health care system.

Before the political and subsequent economic changes in Czechoslovakia in November 1989 the health care system was based on the Soviet model where quantity rather than quality was the dominant factor. Health care was hospital centred, primary care was poorly developed and the system was characterised by a lack of investment.

Following Communist principles, health care workers were paid low wages in line with workers outside the health care sector. Primary care doctors acted generally in a referral role and were not well respected. In order to supplement their income, a system of bribes and gratuities was developed, which despite being illegal, flourished throughout the health care system. Private facilities were not permitted and all facilities belonged to, and were controlled by, the state.

As with the remainder of Europe, health care costs have been steadily escalating. In 1995 health care expenditure topped $3.5 billion. Approximately 8 per cent of the country's income is spent on health care, which is comparable to many western countries in percentage terms, and double the pre-1989 levels. Although this equates to a per capita spend of around $300 (far below that of EU countries), with the Czech economy being one of the fastest growing in Europe, absolute levels of expenditure are expected to rise continually for at least the next decade. The increasingly affluent Czech population of 10 million is expecting better standards of health care, giving rise to demands for better quality and, therefore, more modern and more expensive treatment.

Following the dismantling of the Federation, the two countries proceeded to reform their system of health care in different ways, while still both retaining an insurance-based system. The Czech Republic opted for full-scale privatisation of primary and some secondary care along with most of the pharmaceutical industry including manufacturers, distributors and pharmacies. The insurance scheme was expanded to allow private insurance companies to enter the market and there are now over 20 active insurance companies. Service providers are paid a mixture of a fixed income based on capitation and a 'fee for service'. This system has resulted in many problems, with many loss making and badly administered insurance companies either delaying or defaulting on payments to health care providers.

Pharmaceutical industry

The Czech Republic saw a massive influx of imports from the West since its borders were opened in 1989, and now virtually all the major international pharmaceutical companies have an established presence in the country. Up until 1995, western manufacturers took an increasing proportion of the market in both volume, and more importantly, value terms. This now appears to have stabilised, with – in 1995 – 45 per cent of sales by volume, and 22 per cent by value coming from domestic manufacturers. In 1995, pharmaceutical sales increased 21 per cent over 1994 levels and reached £620 million.

Pre-1990, the Czech pharmaceutical industry was far less developed than that of Hungary, which housed the pharmaceutical research and manufacturing base of the COMECON countries. In the Czech Republic, five main companies were grouped under the control of SPOFA, the state pharmaceutical company. SPOFA allocated products and production schedules to each company, set prices, and organised selling and distribution. All competition was kept to a minimum and surplus profits were reallocated to other areas rather than being reinvested in the industry.

On 1 October 1995, the Czech Republic introduced a new reimbursement scheme for pharmaceuticals which is based on the cost of the active substance rather than on the finished product price. It was the intention of the Ministry of Health to fix prices based on the cheapest available form of each drug, with the aim of curtailing the spiralling drugs bill.

Today, the domestic pharmaceutical industry by international standards is very small. For example, the largest pharmaceutical company, Leciva, is expected to post 1996 profits of circa £15 million: a drop in the ocean compared to the Glaxos of this world. All the leading domestic pharmaceutical companies are represented by the Czech Pharmaceutical Association, which was formed in 1993. The three main Czech pharmaceutical manufacturers are in different stages of ownership. Galena, the second largest, has so far been the only one to successfully attract international attention and was purchased in 1994 by IVAX, a generic manufacturer based in North America. Both Leciva and Lachema are majority owned by the National Property Fund, having had their shares transferred to the Fund prior to being offered for sale. All three companies benefited from the new reimbursement system, although Galena probably emerged in the best position with its product range being most favoured by the new scheme.

Medical equipment opportunities

Continued privatisation and commercialisation of the health care service has resulted in an increased demand for medical equipment. Before 1990, due to the lack of investment, much of the medical equipment was antiquated. The 1990s has seen a growing demand for more modern equipment, particularly from private doctors and laboratories. The greatest growth in demand has been for disposable supplies and relatively low-technology equipment. With the ongoing privatisation of hospitals, the market for larger, more sophisticated equipment will also start to take off.

For western suppliers, the 1990s saw the Czech market totally opened up to overseas companies. Virtually every major pharmaceutical, medical equipment and disposable product company has established sales and marketing operations in the country. Each has gone recognising that, although the current market is only limited, the burgeoning economy and growing health care expenditure will mean greater rewards for those companies that were in there early on. These companies are already starting to reap the commercial benefits of being in early; they have become familiar with the fairly arduous registration and testing procedures, have garnered experience of market conditions, have developed brand awareness and have built the necessary commercial relations with the country's key health care decision makers. While it is never too late to enter any market, for those companies that have not already entered into the Czech Republic it is becoming increasingly more difficult and expensive to do so. The days of cheap take-over targets and competition against unsophisticated domestic companies have passed. The message is very much one of *Get Established Soon* – otherwise the Czech market for many medical product areas will be dominated by those others who moved faster.

23

Tourism

Cerrex Ltd

Tourism has been one of the country's major sources of foreign exchange and a counterweight to its growing trade deficit. The sector accounted for 5.5 per cent of the Czech GDP in 1994 and earnings were equivalent to some 15 per cent of value of Czech exports – a five-fold increase on the 1990 figures. It has provided a crucial source of new jobs to balance declining employment in manufacturing. During 1996, tourism in the Czech Republic received a considerable publicity boost as a result of high-profile visitors like the Michael Jackson tour in early September, and the country reaching the final of the European football championship. This has, for example, stimulated a doubling of the flights from Manchester and the launching of day-trips to Prague. The country remains very inexpensive, although to the traveller, prices appear to have doubled in the past five years. Standards of accommodation and food are increasing – Egon Ronay's *Seagram Guide* for 1996 lists Prague's V. Zatisi as the best Eastern European restaurant.

Official Czech figures show an average of 100 million people per year visiting the Czech Republic in 1994–1996, the vast majority of whom were day trippers only or cross-border workers. Some 17 million stayed overnight averaging about 4.1 days. More than half of these went to Prague only – about four times the number of those staying in South Moravia and in West Bohemia, the two second most popular areas. Outside Prague, the most visited cities were Kelnik, Ceske Budjovice and Karlovy Vary in West Bohemia.

Recent trends show a steady increase in wealthier tourists and increased expenditure per head of 20 per cent between 1995 and 1996, (after allowing for inflation and the increased price of rooms). Private accommodation appears to be declining as tourist demands become more sophisticated. The number of travel agents has halved over the past four years and looks as though it will decline further. CEDOK, the former state travel agency now owned by Unimex, the Austrian duty-free goods group, has seen its international market share fall to about 17 per cent although maintaining about 30 per cent of the domestic market, and they are no longer hotel owners.

Table 23.1 Tourist trends in the Czech Republic

	1992	1993	1994	1995	1996 (estimate)
Total number of visitors [3] (millions)	69.4[1]	71.7[1]	101.1	98.1	105
Total number of staying tourists (millions)	11.1	11.5	17.0	16.5	17.2
Foreign currency earned from tourism ($billion)	1.1	1.6	1.97	2.9	3.8[2]

(1) excludes visitors from Slovakia

(2) Projection for 1997 is $4 billion. Some 80 per cent of revenue comes from tourists to Prague

(3) All persons crossing the borders including workers from Poland and Slovakia who cross the border daily, and day trippers. *Source*: Ministry of the Economy

Investment

Investment in tourism to date has been higher than in any other branch of the economy. If growth in that sector is to be sustained, more investment is required in road, airport and rail networks and in the quality of tourist facilities on offer. Main priorities to date have been the construction of hotels geared to the business and wealthier travellers – there is no longer a shortage of 5 star and 4 star accommodation in Prague – and foreign interest and involvement in hotels (Swiss, French, UK and USA–Hilton, Intercontinental) is strong, as well as projects aimed at extending the length of stay of tourists and visitors including sporting and club facilities. A programme to modernise the hotels of 60 – 90 years old is continuing.

The Czech government has adopted a *laissez faire* attitude towards the tourist industry. Responsibility at government level has traditionally been with the Ministry of the Economy, with the Czech Tourist Authority responsible for elements such as publicity and promotion, some of which is also undertaken by the town halls and local regions. Little central government funding has been made directly available except for the funding of the Czech Tourist Authority, although tourism has benefited from government expenditure in environment and infrastructure. Whether this policy will change as a result of the transfer of responsibility for tourism to the Ministry for the Development of Regions Towns and Communities remains to be seen. Government licensing of some activities in the leisure sector is in force, but the standards to be met are not strict. A new law has been prepared based more closely on European standards, including minimum standard of service, and the need to improve the standard offered by travel agencies and guides.

Future developments

Best future prospects probably lie in the middle range hotels, where demand is growing considerably in the outskirts of the main cities and hotels/motels along the highway. Spa towns are prime locations for joint ventures, cinemas, theatres, cultural sites, sporting facilities/ski resorts and golf courses, spas and casinos. All provide opportunities for development and modernisation which, unless there is a change in government policy, will need to be funded by private enterprise, possibly in combination with local regional authorities.

Lack of domestic sources of funds have made developments outside Prague more difficult. The capital required to finance a 15-bedroom hotel outside Prague, for example, is too great for most regional authorities to raise by themselves. Townships and regions have cooperated to raise the capital to undertake joint ventures with foreign organisations. Joint venture proposals put forward by the Czech authorities and those looking for foreign capital are published regularly in the *Catalogue of Municipal and Regional Projects*.

The Czech Tourist Office (CCC) has been conducting continuous campaigns to strengthen the position of the Czech regions. The authority set out with the aim of improving cooperation between the regions and publicising the Golden Ring of south West and Central Bohemia, tours of religious relics, and a tour of Bohemia's and Moravia's chateaux and castles. New agencies have been set up for each area and local authorities are making financial provision to encourage tourism. Ceske Budjovice local authority, for example, increased spending on publications more than tenfold in 1996. A tourism promotion body covering Southern Bohemia has been established. In 1996 Plzen staged a series of events to mark the town's 700th anniversary. A group of local authorities including Hradec Kralove, Cesky Krumlov, Telc and Kulna Hora have set up 'Ceska Inspirace' to promote themselves at major foreign events.

Some institutional foreign investment has entered the country, for example UNDP grants aimed at small and medium enterprises, the establishment of a model regional tourist development at Ceske Raj (Czech Paradise), the setting up of regional and local databases along European standards (Project Amadeus) and for revitalisation of town 'showpieces'. EU financial assistance has gone towards surveying the 'crossborder' prospects around Lake Lipno near the borders with Germany and Austria – formerly a military 'excluded area' and where the area is ripe for green field development.

The immediate targets for the tourist sector are to ensure that the greater proportion of those coming over the border stay for one night or longer, and to encourage tourists away from Prague, Charles Bridge and the Old Town Square, that are already under pressure, to go to other cities such as Telc and Cesky Krumlov, already in the UNESCO list of historical monuments. The first does not appear to be unattainable bearing in mind the levels of tourism the country has to offer. The infrastructure is being improved throughout the country – for example, the new terminal at the city airport and historical monuments are receiving new signs.

There are plans for a 170 sq km recreational and tourist area in the district of Ceska Lipe sponsored by the mayors of Ralsko and Mimon. This would supplement the established attractions of the area such as Karlovy Vary. A second area into which foreign investment interest is expected to be encouraged is in the south-west of Ceske Krumlov around Lake Lipno. Government assistance in these two areas, plus the area around Plzen to the west of Prague, is expected to be only in the area of infrastructure development – building of main routes to these areas, ecological improvement and publicity. A complex is planned by travel agencies from Belgium and the Netherlands near the town of Pelhrimov to help open up the Czech Moravian uplands. Other targets of investment would be improvement of the infrastructure in Western Bohemia, centred on Plzen and bordering Germany, attracting a large number of tourists from Germany and which contains many of the country's most famous spa towns (Karlovy Vary, Frantiskovy Lazne, Marianske Lazne).

BCSA

British Czech and Slovak Association

The BCSA is established to advance the education of the public in matters relating to the history, politics, science, economies, arts and literature of Britain and the Czech and Slovak Republics. It encourages and facilitates the development of contacts at personal, institutional and corporate levels through a variety of educational, social and business circle events programme, a regular members' newsletter and an annual dinner.
The BCSA is a registered charity and the membership consists of individuals, families, institutions and companies.
New members are always welcome.

For further information please contact:

Jitka Paterson Sigmund, Membership Secretary
British Czech and Slovak Association
522 Finchley Road, London NW11 8DD
Telephone 0181-458 1777
Registered Charity No: 1049411

Part 3

Business Development

24

Market Intelligence

VP International

The days when any economic information was treated as a highly classified state secret are now long gone. With regards to obtaining business information, there are now so many and varied sources, it is more of a problem determining which are the *best* sources. Information about business in the Czech Republic abounds; even the Czech President has his own web site. For those who have not yet mastered the nuances and intricacies of the Czech language, fear not, extensive information is also available in English. This chapter, in no order of preference or prejudice, details the variety of places and organisations that can provide information on the Czech Republic. Many of the UK ones cover not only the Czech Republic, but are pertinent for the whole of Central and Eastern Europe.

UK Government sources

The DTI is having a major, and very welcome, push on business in the region. Its Central Europe Campaign, starting in January 1997, will run for an 18 month period covering five Central European countries including the Czech Republic. The objectives of the campaign are to raise the level of general awareness of the markets among UK companies and to target the specific opportunities that exist in five sectors. Those sectors are:

1   automotive
2   consumer goods and retailing
3   electronics and telecomms
4   health care
5   agri-business.

As its name suggests, The East European Trade Council has one of the best business libraries in this country and cooperative staff who know the region well. It is worth spending a day browsing through its extensive Czech section and its bi-monthly *Bulletin* details events and information pertaining to the region.

The British Embassy tends to be very helpful but again usually has only limited specific information and time for individual companies: however, it is very good for pointing in the right direction. The British Embassy will give a list of all the UK companies based in the Czech Republic and very useful advice can be obtained from making contacts with those UK firms that are already established.

Czech Government

The Czech Embassy's commercial section is a good starting point. If starting up manufacture is the objective, try the investment agency: CzechInvest provides comprehensive advice and assistance for any overseas company which intends to invest in manufacturing.

Consultants, lawyers *et al*

Consultants advising on how to do business in the country are plentiful, both UK or Czech based. All the major management consultancy and law firms are very well represented throughout the Czech Republic, plus numerous others large and small, domestic and international. Many produce business guides of varying degrees of depth and content. Market research firms also abound. If you wish to commission professional organisations to assist you, the British Embassy can provide information on where to find them.

Magazines and journals

English language publications can be divided into those that cover Central Europe and those that are specifically Czech. Regional publications include *The Economist*'s *Business Central Europe*, *Business Europa* and *The Wall Street Journal*'s *Central European Economic Review*. The *Central European Business Weekly* is a weekly newspaper with a Czech bias.

The Prague Business Journal is published weekly and is a very good source of quality, up to date business information. *The Prague Tribune* is a monthly magazine devoted to business issues. The Czech Ministry of Trade also produces a detailed monthly business magazine, *Czech Business and Trade*, which is good for identifying agents/distributors. The weekly *Prague Post* covers all news aspects, but also has reasonable business coverage. Both *The Prague Business Journal* and *The Prague Tribune* produce an annual 'Book of Lists' which is just that;

list upon list of the largest companies in particular industry sectors, with addresses and named contacts.

Aspekt is a publishing company providing a wide variety of stock market monitoring services and produces financial analyses of various industry sectors on a regular basis. If you are looking for four walls of any sort, *Estates News* is the definitive monthly publication covering all aspects of the property world, both residential and commercial.

A business press cuttings service based on scanning the region's English language press is provided by VP International.

Directories, databases and CD Roms

Several business directories listing major Czech firms are available. Inform Katalog and Kompass are the two most widely-known directories with entries on several thousand of the largest firms. Max Business Adviser is a CD which gives comprehensive details not only on the largest firms, but has various legal, trade and economic information. The PP Agency has produced a CD of major companies. Dun and Bradstreet produces an annual publication, 'Major Companies of Central and Eastern Europe', which lists 1,200 companies in the Czech Republic. If your fingers feel like doing some walking, *Golden Pages* is the Czech equivalent of our beloved *Yellow Pages* and has an English index. Recently the EBRD has produced a directory of business information sources for the region. Tradelinks provides, in book form, translations into English of all the Czech commercial laws.

Internet

Numerous business internet sites pertaining to the region and the country have sprung up. If you fancy e-mailing Vaclav Havel at the Presidential Office, surf over to his web site and view various of his recent speeches translated into four languages. The best business internet site on the region is that run by Internet Securities, which has many of the region's leading publications and databases. Other regional business web sites include that of the Central Europe on-line, the EBRD and VP International.

Virtually all the business publications pertaining to the region now have their own web sites. If you want to surf the Internet for market research, it is well worth running up the phone bill. There is a lot of quality information ranging from relevant business articles to contacts; all available for those that have a few hours to peer at a green screen and wander around cyberspace.

Exhibitions

The equivalent of the UK's NEC is Brno. This is an excellent place to undertake specific market research or find agents/distributors. The exhibition catalogues can become your Bible. Some very good specialist exhibitions have now emerged in Prague (at the Vystaviste exhibition ground) and several of these are starting to rival the longer established Brno ones.

Conferences

Numerous conferences on every business topic under the sun are organised regularly; many of the regional ones are based in Prague. Some of the main organisers are Adam Smith Institute and Euroforum.

Publications and reports

Business reports on diverse topics are available at a price. Good ones are worth every penny of the three to four figures that they may cost. The *Financial Times* Management Reports Division and *The Economist* are two of the leading producers of these. Occasionally various trade associations have commissioned specific reports on their particular sector.

Et al

The EBRD has extensive pertinent information which it offers on a subscription basis. VP International has an extensive array of commercial information on the Czech Republic at its Chester office. The Czech National Chamber has a British section and endeavours to assist UK companies. The British Czech and Slovak Association aims to encourage the development of contacts at personal, institutional and corporate levels, through an active events programme and a regular newsletter.

Very occasional jewels can be UK trade associations and local chambers. From experience most have very limited and/or very dated information. The same applies to the majority of business school and other commercial libraries. Trade missions organised by some of the chambers are a cost-effective means for an initial sounding out of the Czech market.

Summary

The more information, the greater the reduction of risk. In isolation, none of the sources detailed above is likely to give you all the information you need. However, by going to several of the sources whose addresses can be found in Appendix II, a company should be able to derive sufficient and reliable information of Czech market conditions on which to determine future actions.

Essential books for the world's market leaders
Forthcoming International Business Books from
Kogan Page

Doing Business with South Africa

Third Edition
Consulting Editors:
Jonathan Reuvid and Ian Priestner

£40.00 Paperback
ISBN 0 7494 2125 8
350 Pages March 1997
Order ref: KT125

"An outstanding publication..." JOHANNESBURG STOCK EXCHANGE

"Well researched, comprehensive and useful"
SIR LEON BRITTAIN, EU COMMISSIONER

The guide covers all aspects of business in South Africa, its "best practice", foreign and internal investment opportunities, and includes an invaluable profile of corperate development since the elections. This latest edition is an essential guide for those businesses dealing with the complex South African markets.

Doing Business in with Germany

Published for the German-Brit Chamber of Industry & Comm
In association with Clifford Chance, Coopers & Lybrand ar
Lufthansa

£18.99 Paperback
ISBN 0 7494 2152 5
February 1997
Order ref: KT152

An invaluable guide, Doing Business with Germany provides t comprehensive information that potential international partners wo need to know before getting involved with a German firm, as well information for German companies seeking co-operative strategies v foreign companies in Germany.

An essential overview and reference handbook for corpo managers, entrepreneurs, investors, bankers and professional adviser

Other bestselling titles in Kogan Page's Doing Business series include:

Doing Business with North America
£35.00 Paperback
ISBN 0 7494 1240 2
Order ref: KS240

Doing Business with Spain
£18.99 Paperback
ISBN 0 7494 1918 0
Order ref: KS918

Doing Business with Latin America
£35.00 Paperback
ISBN 0 7494 1825 7
Order ref: KS825

Doing Business with China
£75.00 Paperback
ISBN 0 7494 1204 6
Order ref: KS204

The Strategic Guide to International Trade

Consultant Editor: Jonathan Reuvid

A unique publication combining in-depth and up-to-date information with a range of strategies for cor ate advancement. The guide covers patterns and trends in world trade and investment; legal elements in the V the significance of both GATT and NAFTA and the framework and specific practices of international trade.
Providing a clear and accessible survey of the new world trading order, the guide is an invaluable reso for senior executives and finance directors trading in the international markets.

£35.00 Paperback
ISBN 0 7494 1621 1
350 Pages December 1996
Order ref: KS621

CBI European Business Handbook 1997

Fourth Edition
Consultant Editor:
Adam Jolly

£35.00 Paperback
January 1997
ISBN 0 7494 2088 X
Order ref: KT088

"...this handbook should be on your desk, not on your shopping list. This has to be the best value for money for a handbook of this type for a long while."

SALES AND MARKETING MANAGEMENT JOURNAL

With an expert analysis of the business, economic and political prospects in 26 European countries, the CBI European Business Handbook is the ideal source book for trading and investment in the new Europe.

The Export Handbook 1997

Fourth Edition
Consultant Editor:
Harry Twells

£30.00 Paperback
May 1997
ISBN 0 7494 2157 6
Order ref: KT157

Completely revised and updated the handbook contains practical advice on how to export successfully to the world's major trade areas including principles of exporting; export opportunities and difficulties in the European Single Market; contacts and advice for export trading; and a unique directory of export services.

A detailed directory and a new section indicating the best places to go for further information and advice make, The Export Handbook 1997 an invaluable reference source for anyone wishing to carve a niche in international markets, and vital reading for all students of international trade.

International Executive Development Programmes

Second Edition
Consultant Editor:
Philip Sadler

£75.00 Paperback
January 1997
ISBN 0 7494 1625 4
Order ref: KS625

The guide is the only truly international guide and directory of international development programmes - invaluable to those businesses that view human development as an ongoing part of essential business practice.

With editorial overviews from some of the world's leading companies and bodies, a comprehensive reference section and an extensive profile of business schools and management centres worldwide, the guide provides you with all the information you need to transform your managment and hence your business capabilities.

Germany's Top 500

In association with
Frankfurter Allgemeine
Zeitung

£90.00 Paperback
December 1996
ISBN 3 929368 38 2

A unique single information source to evaluate and compare the performance and structure of germany's major companies banks and insurers. Updated annually the guide profiles the companies' addresses, full names, business activities, shareholders, share earnings, dividends and equity and fully comprehensive financial reports over four consecutive years.

Germany's Top 500 is the most complete, authoritative, English-language reference book on German companies, giving you all the information you require to evaluate the performance of a single company or an entire industry.

More information on these and other titles can be found in Kogan Page's comprehensive *International Business Catalogue*. To request a copy please phone or fax the marketing department on:

Tel. 0171 278 0433 Fax. 0171 837 6348.

Kogan Page's *international business books* can be brought from good booksellers or direct from Kogan Page's customer services department on 0171 278 0433, quoting the reference number for the title and your credit card details.

Payment can also be made by pro-forma, or by cheque made out to Kogan Page Ltd and sent to: Kogan Page, 120 Pentonville Road, London N1 9JN, England

25

Trade and Project Finance

Kevin R Smith, AWS Corporate Finance & Consultancy

The finance of trade with the Czech Republic has undergone a number of fundamental and rapid changes in the last decade. Before the break up of the Eastern bloc in 1989 and the disbanding of the COMECON in 1991, UK exporters only had to deal with a very limited number of Foreign Trade Organizations (FTOs) and the monopolistic state owned banks responsible for all foreign trade. Both the FTOs and the state banks were able to demonstrate a long track record and the risk was essentially a sovereign one.

With the emergence of the Czech Republic as a separate trading nation came more freedom to trade but greater risks. The UK exporter went from dealing with established, state owned organisations to dealing with newly established companies and banks with no track record and often very little experience of international trade or a market economy.

Initially the risk of default by a Czech company had to be considered very seriously. Even if payment was guaranteed by a local bank these were often no easier to asses or necessarily a better risk.

Many UK companies found that ECGD or EBRD assistance was either not appropriate, too expensive or not available other than for large projects with long lead times and as such the vast majority of business relied on solutions from commercial banks.

As with any developing country, the first trades in a new market or with a new buyer should be conducted using Letters of Credit confirmed or discounted by an acceptable western bank. In the early days this could prove difficult to obtain and quite expensive.

However, as the Czech Republic has proven to be the most dynamic of the emerging markets in Central and Eastern Europe the majority of the difficulties and risks faced by a UK company wishing to trade in the country have reduced significantly. The companies and banks have developed a track record, accounts are often audited to western standards, and experience of international trade and a market economy has been gained very quickly. Political risks are now considered to be perfectly acceptable and finance has become far more widely available and much cheaper.

Methods of payment

The terms of trade are now very similar to trading with a country in Western Europe although it is advisable to remain cautious when dealing with small companies and banks.

Letters of Credit: The larger Czech banks are normally regarded to be a perfectly acceptable payment risk and do not strictly need to be confirmed by a western bank although this often depends upon the UK company's experience and policy. Once a favorable track record has been established other payment methods can be considered.

Bills of Exchange and Promissory Notes: These are often used to finance medium term credit with a stream of bills with maturities every six months. The bills would often carry a bank aval (guarantee) although this may not be necessary for larger companies. The exporter can also ask a bank to discount the bills on a non-recourse basis (a forfait) thus ensuring payment. Forfaiting, until recently the main method of financing medium term trade throughout Central Europe, is declining in importance as foreign companies become more confident in trading in the country.

Open Account: Approximately 90 per cent of all trade in the EU is conducted on an open account basis although many companies have some form of credit insurance. Trade with the Czech Republic is already very close to this figure. Longer term credit for capital goods may still require an L/C or bank avalised bills depending upon the buyer and the value of equipment.

Leasing: Capital goods can now be leased and in the majority of cases there are tax incentives for the buyer. Typically, exporters would sell equipment for cash to a leasing company which then assumes all payment risk. At present structures can still be rather rigid.

Foreign Exchange: The Czech Koruna only became fully convertible in 1995 although foreign exchange transactions were possible previously and the exchange rate has been stable for many years. Most exporters continue to invoice in US dollars or Deutsche marks with some in sterling or Swiss francs. This, together with the stability of the currency means that the foreign exchange rate risks are no greater than for trading with any Western European country.

To summarise, doing business with the Czech Republic has undergone significant changes in the last ten years but there can be no doubting that the risks and the costs are now lower than at any other time in that period. Without exception, the normal trade and project finance options that would be available in trade with Western Europe are now available in trade with the Czech Republic. If new to the country it pays to be cautious and to seek assistance from someone who knows the market especially if dealing with smaller companies or banks.

26

Financial Assistance

Cerrex Ltd*

This section looks at some of the major international and UK assistance funds available to the UK industry wishing to do business in the Czech market. It does not cover other national aid funds – those from Scandinavia and Japan Eximbank, for example – which may offer a mixture of 'tied' and 'untied' aid. With the increasing availability of domestic capital and the increasing strength of the Czech economy, some donors, eg USAID, have stated their intention to reduce their aid commitments to the Republic. The Czech Republic has expressed no wish to receive World Bank loans, although the Bank is willing to continue funding. Nevertheless, as indicated below, there are a large number of aid schemes available.

The Phare Programme

Assistance under the Phare Programme takes the form of support for investment such as studies, capital grants, guarantees and credit lines, infrastructure investment and transfer of know-how including policy advice, technical expertise, training, consultancy work, advice on the development of legislation and institutions.

Phare activities in the Czech Republic focus on preparing the country for entry into the European Union. Targeted areas for the period 1995–1999 include:

- legislative integration;

- institutional integration, focusing on the reform of public administration to ensure that Czech public services meet EU standards, and to help institutions key to the market economy (eg customs, standards);

- infrastructure integration, including the provision of funds for trans-European and cross-border communications links;

* The author acknowledges the assistance of Simon Potter in the preparation of this chapter.

- social and economic development in areas where there is a role for public support, eg SME, export and regional development, the agricultural and energy sectors, employment services, social insurance and management training;
- the promotion of foreign investment through the CzechInvest agency.

A 'Technical Assistance Fund' makes funding available for projects supported by the government but not covered by individual sector programmes.

Aid is also available in the form of a number of multi-country programmes – notably the programmes for cross-border cooperation, active in Western and Northern Bohemia (areas adjacent to Germany and Austria). Seven priority areas include:

1. the transport sector, for the improvement of the Decin-Prague-Breclav railway line and a number of E-roads;

2. the energy sector, aimed at reducing energy consumption and pollution and modernising supply systems;

3. the rehabilitation of historical monuments;

4. aid to sewage disposal and treatment, waste management and treatment of toxic soil.;

5. the removal of barriers to economic development in the area, and the creation of a sound infrastructure and health private sector;

6. the diversification of agricultural incomes and the promotion of cross-border cooperation in rural development and marketing;

7. cross-border cooperation in employment schemes and vocational training.

Companies interested are advised to approach the Project Management Units (PMUs) in the various sectors. Other key personnel to be approached include the local industries and trade associations in the Republic and companies which can form the 'local expert element' needed for the contracts, aid coordinators within the EU delegation in Prague, and relevant contacts in the 'country' and 'industry' desks in the European Commission.

Most contracts are put out to open tender, although PMUs have the discretionary powers to award contracts up to about 40,000 ECU without going through full tendering procedures. UK companies working closely with the relevant Czech organisations and PMUs in the Czech Republic can also initiate projects. Phare aims to allocate contracts among member states broadly in proportion to budget allocations. At present the UK is winning more than its 'fair share' of contracts and UK companies will have a greater chance of winning contracts if they present proposals in cooperation with companies based in southern Europe.

Registration on the Phare Central Consultancy Register (CCR) is necessary for firms that wish to receive details of projects on a regular basis and provide services or supplies within the programme. For more information, UK companies should contact the Phare Information Office and the DTI's World Aid Section, whose database contains details of projects and programmes already funded under Phare.

The Joint Venture Phare Programme (JOPP)

A part of the main EC Programme, JOPP encourages external investment by EU firms, primarily SMEs, wishing to launch joint ventures with Czech firms.

JOPP offers support to joint ventures:

- at the preliminary stage, the programme can help fund market analysis, business plans, contract negotiations, production of prototypes, pilot projects and pre-feasibility studies;

- at the co-financing stage, JOPP provides medium- to long-term finance for joint ventures, on condition that other investors make similar commitments;

- at the technical assistance phase, the programme provides up to 50 per cent of the eligible costs of transferring know-how to the workforce up to a maximum of ECU 150,000.

The European Bank for Reconstruction and Development (EBRD)

The EBRD seeks to encourage the development of a healthy private sector in the Czech Republic. It concentrates on the restructuring and modernisation of large enterprises and supports SMEs and joint ventures with foreign partners. It normally provides up to 35 per cent of the total cost of a given project through loans, equity and guarantees and underwriting financing, all at commercial rates. EBRD projects also create demand for suppliers and consultants, and contracts open to British firms are advertised in its *Procurement Opportunities* monthly newsletter.

In the Czech Republic, the Bank is particularly involved in finance and banking, energy and telecommunications and in funding environmental schemes, although other sectors are considered. Current commitments include:

- public projects in the telecommunications, airlines and railways sectors;

- eight regional projects, concentrating on SME support, finance and telecommunications;

- eighteen technical cooperation programmes aimed at project preparation and support in motorways, telecommunications, banking, energy, chemicals, manufacturing, agriculture, wholesale markets, institutional and regional development, business planning, energy efficiency and the environment.

These priorities are not set to change radically – EBRD projects in the near future will concentrate on banking and finance, energy saving and textiles.

The European Investment Bank (EIB)

The European Investment Bank operates on a non-profit basis. It offers know-how, support and loans, at a preferential rate. The loans largely take the form of joint funding, with the EIB offering up to 50 per cent of project costs and working in conjunction with other bodies such as the EBRD. Small and medium-sized enterprises require third-party bank guarantees.

The EIB's priority sectors include transport and telecommunications, the restructuring and modernisation of the energy sector, and joint ventures and direct investments by EU firms in industry. Recent loans to the Czech Republic have included finance for small- and medium- scale manufacturing and tourism projects, modernisation of the transport and telecommunications networks, and upgrading of lignite-fired power stations.

The International Finance Corporation (IFC)

The IFC's priorities include:

- aiding the establishment of joint ventures with foreign partners;

- assisting in privatisation and other reforms;

- modernisation of privatised industry;

- helping to transform the financial sector and build sound capital market institutions;

- assisting small and medium-sized firms by creating suitable financial intermediaries.

The IFC operates in three main ways:

1. Financing private sector activity through loans of between $1m and $100m equity, investments of up to 35 per cent of a company's share capital, and lines of credit etc for SMEs through intermediary institutions (local commercial banks etc). Unlike, for example, the EIB, the IFC charges market rates.

2. Helping companies to mobilise financing in the international financial markets. The IFC acts primarily as a catalyst, providing a maximum of 25 per cent of financing for any single project, but using its reputation as an endorsement to increase investor confidence and encourage private sector investment.

3. Providing advice and technical assistance on financial packages, corporate restructuring, privatisation, formulation of business plans and identification of markets, products, technologies and financial and technical partners. Much of this is carried out through the IFC's Technical Assistance Trust Fund.

The United Nations

While the UN does not offer aid *per se* to those wishing to do business in the Czech Republic, its various agencies have extensive procurement needs in the country, and tenders are often open to British firms. The most important source of contracts is the United Nations Industrial Development Organisation (UNIDO) which carries out industrial studies and encourages the 'UNIDO Roster of Consulting Organisations', while equipment suppliers should complete the 'Questionnaire for UNIDO Roster of Vendors'. There is a UK Investment promotion coordinator at UNIDO whose role is to identify opportunities for British companies.

CzechInvest

CzechInvest's purpose is to encourage foreign investment in the country targeting 'greenfield' and joint ventures. Presently its main priorities are automobiles, electronics and precision engineering, although the priority areas could expand during 1997 to include chemicals among others. CzechInvest offers potential investors a number of free services:

1. Investment data, and information on doing business in the Czech Republic. Brief sector reports are also provided.

2. Assistance in the organisation of visits, and help in dealing with government organisations.

3. Aid in managing the investment process.

CzechInvest is divided into four departments, each with its own function:

- The 'Greenfield Projects division' offers help in the search for sites for new development, in the construction and recruitment phases, and during any subsequent expansion.

- The Joint Ventures section maintains a database of Czech companies interested in foreign cooperation, which can be matched with British firms, and can also offer help in choosing a location and negotiating procedures.

- The Regions Department uses CzechInvest's network of local representative offices to pinpoint suitable sites and help foreign companies with the implementation of investment plans.

- The Marketing and Public Relations Department maintains contact with the media, prepares presentations for potential investors, and manages direct marketing programmes.

Department of Trade and Industry (DTI)

The DTI, as well as jointly running the Know-How Fund (see below) administers a number of other help programmes for those wishing to do business with the Czech Republic.

1. The Overseas Project Fund administered by the Projects Export Promotion Division makes aid available to UK companies pursuing contracts which could lead to a supply of UK goods or services worth more than £50m. Financial help can offset the cost of feasibility studies, consultancy fees etc – the exact amount depends on the content, duration and potential benefits of the project.

2. The HOTS (Hands-on Training Scheme for Overseas Decision Makers) helps British firms bring Czech citizens with influence in procurement decisions to the UK to learn about UK technology, industrial practices and management techniques. It is up to the individual firm to nominate suitable candidates and to propose the type of training that they will undergo. If the DTI endorses the choice, it will refund up to half of the approved costs.

3. Financial aid is also available to companies wishing to become part of a trade mission organised and sponsored by a trade association or similar body.

The Know-How Fund (KHF)

In the Czech republic, the 'Know-How Fund' has focused on banking and finance (about half of the KHF's Czech funds have been spent on the financial sector), public administration and local government, management training and SME development. Much of the Fund's activity is now directed towards smaller scale activities, including encouragement of study visits by Czech citizens to the UK, training in banking and the financial sector and in areas related to EU membership such as foreign trade and anti-dumping, training programmes for public servants, the 'Strategic Planning for Prague' initiative and the development of management training capacity. Additional areas include the reduction of regional pockets of high unemployment by offering advice in areas such as youth training, the provision of help for business agencies, and SME development.

Interested British firms should register details of their interests and expertise with the Contracts Branch of the Overseas Development Administration (ODA). The KHF also welcomes proposals for projects, providing that they fall within its priority sectors – applicants should contact the Fund before preparing a detailed proposal. For projects funded entirely by the KHF, competitive tendering is the norm, and disbursements are usually tied to British companies. KHF funds for 1997 are heavily committed.

KHF Investment Schemes

The KHF runs two programmes of interest to those seeking to invest in the Czech Republic. The Pre-Investment Feasibility Studies scheme (PIFS) is available to those firms which have already undertaken basic market research and are considering long-term investment in the Czech Republic and can provide up to 50 per cent of the cost of research into the commercial and financial viability of the project. The Training for Investment Personnel Scheme (TIPS) offers aid to those training Czech investment operations personnel in management and business skills. There has been less competition for these funds than for funding under the main KHF scheme.

British Council

The British Council, with its network of local contacts, educational and cultural events, promotes British companies through the management of sponsored events, financing of a wide range of exchange programmes and even providing funding for those presenting papers at conferences etc. The JICAP (Joint Industrial and Commercial Attachment) Scheme arranges attachment to British firms for Czech senior and middle managers for up to five weeks.

27

Agencies, Distributorships and Franchises

Jan Grozdanovic and Karin Pomaizlova, Seddons Solicitors

Introduction

Since 1989 there has been a big boom in business in the Czech Republic accompanied by numerous investments made by foreign companies. Many of the firms have established branches or subsidiaries in the Czech Republic. However, the establishment of a branch or a subsidiary still remains quite a time-consuming and costly business. As a result some foreign producers prefer to enter the Czech market through selected local agents or distributors. The business environment has changed during the past seven years, with the end of the state monopoly on trade with foreign companies; appointment of agents has now been long established. There are now many private companies in the market searching for foreign expertise and goods in order to set up their own businesses. For the local entrepreneur it is seen as a guarantee of success to cooperate with a well-established foreign company, taking advantage of its good reputation, long history and sophisticated advertising and marketing techniques. However, despite the fact that many agreements have been concluded on the basis of agency, distributorship or franchise, the Czech post-1989 law (including Act No.513/1991 Coll., the Commercial Code) still does not contain any direct provisions on distributorship or franchises. For a foreign entrepreneur it is deemed necessary to conclude an 'innominate contract' (which is a contract not falling within the specific categories governed by the Commercial Code), thus using the general provisions of the Commercial Code. In addition, the general principles to be applied are those of the Civil Code, the Act on Economic Competition and all special laws relevant to the area of business in which the participants wish to operate.

Commercial representation

The relevant provisions of the Commercial Code are paras 652 and the following:

- There is a requirement that the contract shall be concluded in a written form. Under the contract the representative undertakes to perform certain activities leading to the conclusion of various types of contracts on behalf of a principal in return for a commission. Unless otherwise stated in the contract, the representative is not entitled to conclude any such contracts on behalf of the principal unless he is given a power of attorney by the principal.

- The commission shall belong to the representative upon conclusion of an agreement with a third party and after the third party fulfils its obligations under the agreement, unless it was agreed that the representative would only seek opportunities to conclude certain kinds of agreements; then the commission belongs to the representative only after he has found such an opportunity.

- The representative is obliged to assist the principal when concluding such an agreement with a third party, and he guarantees to the principal the fulfilment of obligations of such third party if this formed part of his agreement with the principal.

- The representative is expected to report to the principal on market developments and to provide all other data relevant to the principal's interests. He is obliged to follow the instructions of the principal. If he is empowered to sign agreements on behalf of the principal he is entitled to do so only under the commercial conditions given to him by the principal.

- The representative must not release any information received from the principal or use it for his own benefit if that would be in breach of the interests of the principal.

- Czech law does recognise exclusive and non-exclusive representation. If an exclusive representation agreement is concluded then the principal is to pay a commission to the representative even for contracts which he has signed without his cooperation, unless otherwise agreed.

- The contract may be concluded either for limited or unlimited periods of time. After the expiration of the agreement the representative has a right to a commission for conclusion of contracts if he was instrumental in their conclusion. After expiration of the representation agreement the principal is obliged to pay the representative for customers obtained, if the agreement was terminated one year after its conclusion by the principal. This means that caution must be exercised when selecting a commercial representative.

Agency

The relevant provisions of the Commercial Code governing framework agency agreements are paras 566 and the following:

● The difference between commercial representation and an agency agreement is that a representative acts for a principal for the purpose of arranging certain kinds of agreements, whereas the agent is primarily appointed to arrange one agreement or another matter for the principal. He must do so personally and cannot appoint any other party to carry out his obligations.

● The agent is obliged to act in accordance with the instructions of the principal and advise him of any circumstances which may necessitate a change in his instructions to him. The agreement does not have to be in a written form. However, if the principal requires the agent to conclude any legal transactions on his behalf, he has to furnish the agent with a written power of attorney.

● Unless agreed otherwise, the commission belongs to the agent after the successful conclusion of the matter for the principal. However, unlike in the case of a representation agreement, the agent is not liable and does not guarantee fulfilment of the obligations of a third party unless he undertook to do so.

● If an agency agreement is concluded with an individual, this cannot be considered to be an employment agreement and the relevant person has to have a valid trade licence as a self-employed entrepreneur.

Distributorship

Goods are supplied to the local market by sale of the goods from a foreign manufacturer to a local distributor who at his own cost distributes the goods to the local market. This seems to provide very little risk for the foreign manufacturer. However, what has to be considered is the strength of the local partner and whether the lack of professionalism, capital and experience may adversely affect the goodwill of the manufacturer.

The agreement between the manufacturer and the distributor may be governed by the Commercial Code if the parties do not select the law of the country of the manufacturer as the governing law of their agreement. Their relationship implies certain obligations on the manufacturer to supply non-defective goods, to bear responsibility for defective goods, warranties, delivery obligations, and damage to the goods up until the time they are delivered to the purchaser. However, it seems most important to secure the intellectual property rights of the manufacturer in the area where the goods will be distributed, and also to establish a good service and to set a certain standard for future distribution to avoid subsequent loss of goodwill and deterioration in the quality of goods caused by bad storage, service and repair. Thus it seems feasible to include in the agreement extra provisions which imply the right of the manufacturer to control the quality of sale of his goods and certain standards or marketing tools which should be maintained with the assistance and guidance from the manufacturer. As a result of choosing the wrong distributor, the manufacturer may lose the market even though there may be a demand for his high quality goods.

Before concluding such an agreement, a search of the necessary import licences, import duty and technical standards should be carried out. If required by Czech law, the goods may have to be submitted to the Czech authorities for testing. It is up to the contracting parties to agree on the law which will govern their relationship (as in the previous sections) and also to decide which way subsequent disputes may be resolved. Under the new law on arbitration it is now possible to choose an arbitration court or an arbitrator to resolve a dispute.

Franchising

So far no direct law has been adopted to regulate franchise relationships. However, Czech law, in particular the Commercial Code and the relevant intellectual property laws, provides a general scheme for such relationships. Franchise agreements are concluded as innominate contracts and therefore it is most important to cover in detail every aspect of the prospective relationship otherwise there may not be any protection from the law if the rules are not expressly defined in the agreement.

In addition to the above, franchising represents a relatively low capital risk for the manufacturer or a service provider who wishes to expand into the local market. However, certain tools for control of the goods and services provided need to be maintained as well as the provision of in-depth training on company philosophy and expertise. The choice of a strong local partner is very important as failure by the local franchisee to provide the foreign products or services to a high standard could irreparably damage the company's image and goodwill, leading, potentially, to the loss of the whole market.

It is very important to provide the local franchisee with all relevant technical data as Czech law provides stringent rules on workshops and shops maintenance with regard to environmental protection, hygiene, static and fire safety regulations and so on. It should be ensured that all intellectual property rights of the franchisor are protected under the local law in the relevant market and that appropriate licences are given to the franchisee. All the information and training provided for the franchisee should be protected under the Commercial Code's provisions on unfair competition and breach of business secrecy. Agreement should be reached with the franchisee on the form the standard employment contracts should take to secure quality of work, to maintain confidence and to restrain employees from using the company's expertise to set up businesses in competition with that of their employer. This is now possible based on the recent decision of the Constitutional Court, but it is to be carefully considered in detail since there are limits for preventing employees from carrying out certain activities after their employment has been terminated. To maintain good control over the franchise business, becoming a co-partner in the local company of a franchisee may be recommended. It may also help to build up a stronger capital base for the franchisee, eg by improving the possibility of obtaining bank loans.

In contracts concluded with a local business agent, distributor or franchisee, consideration should be given to the protection of intellectual property rights. A new provision has been adopted into the Trade Marks Act No.137/1995 Coll., which significantly improves the security for foreign companies acting through an agent or representative. Since then it has been practically impossible for an agent or a representative to register a foreign company's trademark and become its owner without the foreign company's consent.

28

Entrepreneurial Activities and Intellectual Property Rights Protection

Jan Grozdanovic and Karin Pomaizlova, Seddons Solicitors

Intellectual property and know-how licensing

One of the possible forms of carrying on business by foreign entrepreneurs on the Czech market is through cooperation with local manufacturers and distributors. Foreign companies conducting business in the Czech Republic will often wish to protect intellectual property or they will want to use inventions or other intellectual property rights, when using Czech companies as producers or distributors of the foreign company's products or services.

Under Czech law intellectual property rights can be passed to third parties or third parties may be given the right to use certain intellectual property rights based on a licence agreement. Some licence agreements have to be registered with the relevant state authority to bring the agreement into effect. The act of registration has a constitutive, not merely declaratory, force.

Licence agreements are generally governed by the provisions of the Commercial Code No. 513/1991 Coll. (as amended). The Commercial Code provides the parties with a considerable freedom as to the content and terms of the relevant licence agreement. However, this also means that the parties must exercise thoroughness for their future contractual relationship because the provisions on licence agreement in the Commercial Code are relatively brief.

The minimum requirement is that the parties agree on the range of the provided licence and must also set up the area for which the licence shall become effective. The contract must be concluded in writing. If specific legal provisions on individual intellectual property rights prescribe the parties to follow extra conditions, these requirements must be contained in the contract, otherwise the parties risk the contract being invalid. In most cases it is required to register the licence agreement with the relevant register and have it authorised by the Intellectual Property Office (IPO). If the duration of the right is dependent on its performance, the licensee is obliged by the law to do so. On the other hand, the licensor is under an obligation to maintain the right during the term of the licence agreement and, if necessary, to take steps to protect the performance of the right of the licensee. By entering into the licence agreement the licensor neither gives up his right to exercise his rights by himself, nor does he give up the right to conclude other licence agreements relating to the same right, unless otherwise agreed between the parties. The licensee is obliged to keep confidential all information and documentation provided by the licensor in connection with the licence unless these become publicly known through no fault of the licensee. The licence agreement may be concluded either for a limited or unlimited term. If the agreement is for an unlimited term then, unless agreed otherwise, the notice period for termination must be at least one year. Such period commences on the first day of the month following the month in which the termination notice was delivered to the other party.

In case of infringement of any intellectual rights, remedy may be obtained through Czech courts; however, court procedures may be rather lengthy and costly. Therefore it would be preferable to make provision in the licence agreement for the resolution of any disputes by arbitration. Alternatively, depending on the governing law of the agreement, it would be possible to submit to the jurisdiction of foreign courts.

Know-how

Czech law does not recognise the term 'know-how' as such, although it is commonly used in general business language. The Commercial Code contains a reference to 'trade secrets'. Know-how can, of course, be transferred to a newly established company or a joint-venture company. Where this happens it is treated as an asset of the company. In such a case the know-how owner gives up his right to use it and it becomes the property of the Czech company. When granting a know-how licence the licensor must be aware that Czech law does not provide any specific requirements and the agreement should be drafted in accordance with general commercial principles. It will be necessary to include clauses on the range and the way of providing the necessary valuable know-how, the control of its usage, training and the duration of the contract. In cases of breach of the know-how owner's rights, the owner may seek protection under the Commercial Code provisions on unfair competition. The know-how owner may at any time request that anybody (not only the know-how user) ceases the wrongful acts against the owner, and provides the owner with adequate compensation including damages for loss. The owner may also request the return of any amount by which the wrongdoer has been unjustly enriched through infringement on his part.

Patents

Patents for inventions are governed by the Act No. 527/1990 Coll. (as amended). The definition and approach to inventions and patents for inventions are in principle broadly identical with those in the Anglo-Saxon legal systems. Czech law protects by patent any inventions which are new, and resulting from inventive thinking and which can be used in an industrial process. Protection afforded to foreigners is guaranteed by international agreements to which the Czech Republic is a party. As the patent law is based on the principle of territoriality, the right to use a patent is governed exclusively by Czech law.

The right to use a patent belongs to the inventor or his legal successor. If the invention was made within the scope of an employee's obligation, the right to use the patent passes to the employer, unless otherwise agreed. However, the right to authorship of the invention remains unaffected. The owner of the patent has got the exclusive right to use the invention, and to agree the use of the invention by other persons. The licence agreement, as well as an agreement on the transfer of the patent, becomes effective in relation to third parties upon its registration in the patent register of the IPO. The right to use the invention based on a licence agreement is established on the day of its acceptance by an interested party. The consequence of such an offer is that the owner pays only half of the administrative fees applicable to the patent.

Contrary to English law, Czech law contains the concept of a 'forced licence'. This means that in the case that an owner does not use the invention for which he owns the patent while he has no reasonable excuse for doing so, or in the case of serious public interest, he may be ordered by the IPO to provide a licence for the patent. This is not, however, possible before the expiry of a four-year period from the date of submitting an application to register the patent.

The invention is protected under patent for 20 years from the date of submission of the application for registration of the patent.

Industrial design

Industrial designs are protected by the law on patents.

The conditions of protection are almost the same as those on protection of inventions. The protection applies for five years, but this may be extended for another five years (subject to a maximum of two extensions). This makes a total protection period of 15 years maximum, commencing on the date of submission of the application to the IPO.

Technical design

In order to accelerate the process of acquisition of protection for inventions and also to provide protection for less technical solutions, Czech law, in the Act No. 478/1992 Coll. (as amended) recognises the so-called 'technical designs' as an alternative to inventions.

As regards conditions of protection, these are almost identical to those of an invention, except that the protection period lasts for only four years and can be extended not more than twice by another three years. There are no licensing obligations if the technical design is not to be in use.

Trademarks

Trademarks are governed by the Act on Trademarks No. 137/1995 Coll. As in the previous cases, registration of a trademark has a constitutive, not merely declaratory, character. Under Czech law, not just any mark can be considered to be a trademark and the user may not obtain any rights to it emerging from a trademark protection unless such mark fulfils all conditions of the law to be suitable to be registered as a trademark. The user of a mark becomes the owner of a trademark upon its registration with the IPO. On the other hand, it is not a condition of a registration that the mark is previously used in the market in connection with goods or services of the applicant. To encourage owners not to use their registered trademarks simply for blocking purposes or storage purposes, the registration of a trademark can be cancelled if the mark has not been used continuously for five years in the market for goods or services for which it had been registered and there is no explanatory reason for doing so.

The Czech trademark law does not recognise service marks as a separate category, but they are understood to be included in the general definition of a trademark. Individual and collective trademarks are defined in the Czech trademark law, but certification marks are not recognised. The protection of trademarks is not based on the first use basis but on the formal principle of the first application for registration.

All applications are published in a bulletin issued by the IPO. Protests against registration may be filed with the IPO within three months after the publication. If no protests are filed or if these are successfully defended and the IPO finds that the application does not contain mistakes, the trademark shall be registered. The owner of the trademark shall then have the exclusive right to use it in connection with his goods or services. Without his consent, nobody can use the identical or a confusingly similar mark for the same type of goods or services for which the trademark is registered. The owner may request the court that anybody infringing his rights shall be prohibited from using such mark, and the goods or services can be withdrawn from the market. The owner of a well-known trademark may enforce such rights against anybody, any goods or services and not only against those of the same kind. The owner has a right to adequate compensation of losses.

The right to use a trademark can be awarded only to subjects which conduct business in the same area and are capable of producing the products or services of the kind for which the trademark has been registered. The scope of rights shall be stated in the licence agreement. The right to use the trademark based on such an agreement commences on the day of its registration with the IPO. The duration of the trademark protection is ten years, and can be extended if necessary for another ten years.

The law allows the provision of trademarks as a pledge under a lien agreement. It also affords protection to foreign trademark owners against their agents in the Czech Republic in a country which is a member state of the Paris Convention. Any such owner may request the court to re-register in his name the trademark which the agent has registered for himself in the Czech Republic.

Mark on the origin of goods

This mark is governed by Act No. 159/1973 Coll. (as amended). It consists of geographical names of a country, region or place, which become generally known as data about a place of the origin of goods, the quality and characteristics of which are exclusively determined by the geographical environment, including natural and human factors. The protection commences on the date of registration with the IPO. The registered mark may be used only by the registered person, and cannot be the subject of a licence. Protection is not limited by time. Foreign entities have got the same rights under rules on reciprocity. In case of infringement, the registered person may demand that the court prohibits its unlawful use and orders the remedy for any wrongdoing.

Copyright

Intellectual property rights include copyright. The relevant law is contained in the Authorship Act No. 35/1965 Coll. (as amended). The concept of copyright under Czech law differs greatly from that in Anglo-Saxon legal systems and from the previous categories, and is based on the informal principle.

Copyright is established for the creator of a fiction, science or art work upon its expression in a sensible form. The right to authorship cannot be passed on to any other party. It contains the right for protection of the work against unauthorised use, the disposition right to the work and the right to consent to its use, and the right to authorship reward. Only the author may transfer the right to use the work. The law contains provisions about agreements on the distribution of the work and some of the types of this agreement, eg the publisher's agreement, the agreement on public performance of the work, the agreement on the distribution of the work by rental of copies of the work, broadcasting by TV or radio. It is necessary to stress that a person who obtains the original of the work or its copies does not obtain the right to use the work unless specifically agreed. The contract on distribution of the work must arrange for the manner of use of the work and limits of its distribution, the time when this happens, author's royalty and cooperation of the author, duration of the agreement and undertaking of the user to perform the distribution of the art at his own cost. Such agreement must be concluded in a written form. The author has the right to demand prohibition of interference into his authorship right, restoration, to claim damages and adequate compensation. The performance of the author's work by other persons does not affect the author's rights. The legal protection lasts for the whole of the author's life and continues for 50 years after his death. The right of authorship, however, is unlimited in time.

As regards any works of art created by an employee when fulfilling his obligation from his employment, the employer may use his work without further consent of the author.

29

The Development of the Transport Infrastructure

Aleš Ždimera, CzechInvest

As the global demand for transportation services continues to grow, the volume of goods transported throughout the European market is projected to grow several times over. The Czech Republic, due to its strategic location, will naturally become the pivotal crossroads for pan-European transit traffic along both the East–West and North–South axes. This situation poses enormous requirements on the development and quality of the transport infrastructure, namely the road network, railroads and air traffic.

Overview

With regard to trans-European connections, further development of the transport infrastructure in the Czech Republic in the immediate future is based upon the Agreement of Association of the Czech Republic to the European Union. The Association Agreement also binds the Czech Republic to ensuing obligations to modernise and build the Trans-European Network (TEN) of multi-modal corridors. The Czech Republic is intersected by Corridor IV (Germany – Prague – Brno – Břeclav – Austria/Slovakia) and the inter-connecting branch of Corridor VI (Poland – Ostrava – Přerov – Břeclav – Austria). The following documents govern the upgrading of these corridors:

1. The European Agreement on Main International Traffic Arteries ('AGR' – *Accord Europeen sur les Grandes Routes de Trafic International* – 1976).

2. The Design of the Trans-European North-South Motorway (TEM – 1977).

3. The European Agreement on Main International Railway Lines (AGC – *Accord Europeen sur les Grandes Lignes Internationales de Chemin de Fer* – 1985).

4.   The Project of Trans-European Railway (TER – 1988).

5.   The European Agreement on Important International Combined Transport Lines and Related Installations (AGTC – *Accord Europeen sur les Grandes Lignes de Transport International Combine et les Installations Connexes* – 1991).

The preparation of the European Agreement on Main Inland Waterways of International Importance (AGN – *Accord Europeen sur les Grandes Voies Navigables d'Importance Internationale*) is currently under way.

Of critical importance to the development of transport infrastructure is its financing. The acknowledged need for its rapid construction and connection to the all-European system requires high financial resources that exceed the realistic potential of the Czech state budget. To fill this financial shortfall, resources from the EU have been committed.

In order to modernise the infrastructure, the transportation sector has received grants from the European Union in the total amount of ECU 71.5 million, namely ECU 50 million for the modernisation of the First Railway Transit Corridor, Děčín – Prague – Břeclav, ECU 10 million for the modernisation of the European road system, and ECU 7.6 million for the upgrading of the railway border crossing in Cheb. Loans from the EIB and EBRD in the total amount of ECU 244.37 million were granted for the modernisation of the railway transit corridors.

Road infrastructure

The basic document governing road development is the Czech Government Resolution No. 631/1993 on the extension of motorways and four-lane roads for motor vehicles in the Czech Republic until the year 2005. This document envisages the completion of approximately 640 kilometres of motorways out of a network totalling 1056 kilometres. Similarly some 510 kilometres of four-lane roads are to be constructed to increase the current network of four-lane roads from the current 300 kilometres to a total length of 810 kilometres. The programme of construction of motorways and four-lane roads is updated annually. The chief priorities in motorway construction include the following projects (see map on page 154):

1.   The D5 Motorway Prague – Pilsen – Rozvadov/Waidhaus – Germany, now in operation between Prague and Ejpovice. The 61-kilometre-long portion between Pilsen and Rozvadov currently under construction will be operational in 1997. The construction of the last part of this route will be launched this year and is to be in operation around the year 2000.

2. The D8 Motorway Prague – Ústí nad Labem – Germany. Fourteen kilometres of the total length are operational. This year, another nine-kilometre section will be put into operation. The entire route is to become operational around the year 2000.

3. The connection of Prague and Brno with Ostrava through the extension of existing motorways and four-lane roads: the R35 speed road between Olomouc and Lipník nad Bečvou, and the R48 speed road between Lipník nad Bečvou and Frýdek-Místek, to be opened to traffic around the year 2000.

4. The continued construction of the by-pass ring around Prague, with a section to be launched in 1997.

Integral to these highway construction projects is the improvement of the border crossings on these networks. The number of border crossing-points is to be increased and the capacity of existing crossings is to be improved.

The road network development will be financed primarily from the state budget. Road users will contribute through the obligatory purchase of windscreen stickers for use on designated roads. These stickers are purchased annually.

In 1996, the construction of motorways will cost some CZK 4.9 billion (US$ 180 m), including the sum of CZK 3.6 billion (US$ 132 m) allocated for the D5 Motorway. Motorway construction will require approximately CZK 93 billion (US$ 3.4 bn) until the year 2007, and the construction of 'roads for motor vehicles' (four-lane roads) an extra CZK 45 billion (US$ 1.6 bn). Additionally, the costs of road by-passes in towns will amount to some CZK 35 billion (US$ 1.3 bn) until the year 2000, including almost CZK 18 billion (US$ 600 m) for the completion of the road ring around Prague.

Railroad infrastructure

Four railroad routes along the transit corridors have priority for development:

1. Germany – Děčín – Prague – Česká Třebová – Brno – Břeclav – Austria/Slovakia.

2. Poland – Ostrava – Přerov – Břeclav – Austria.

3. Germany – Cheb/Domažlice – Pilsen – Prague – Česká Třebová – Přerov – Ostrava – Poland/ Slovakia.

4. Germany – Děčín – Prague – Veselí nad Lužnicí – Horní Dvořiště/České Velenice – Austria.

These corridors will be modernised to allow speeds up to 160 km/h, or optimised for the speed of 120 km/h (especially along Corridors 3 and 4) and for the provision of the railway track load capacity of 22.5 metric tons per axle. Out of the current railway track construction length in excess of 9439 kilometres, the speed of 120 km/h is allowed only along 473 kms of the track, and the speed of 140 km/h only along 48 kms of track.

For Corridors 1 and 2, the government has approved the relevant projects, including their financing based on the most favourable government-guaranteed loans, direct subsidies from the state budget as well as direct funding by Czech Railways. The modernisation of Corridor 1 was launched in 1994 and will be completed by 2000. The first three sections will be completed by the end of this year.

The modernisation of Corridor 2 will be launched this year and be completed by 2003.

The feasibility study for the modernisation of Corridor 3 is currently under way and the preliminary feasibility study for Corridor 4 has been completed. Their upgrading is expected to be completed by 2007.

Besides the transit corridors, capital investments are directed also to other routes of the Czech Railways network and the relevant equipment, as part of their reconstruction and safety of operation programme. This year, approximately CZK 1.2 billion (US$ 44 m) will be allocated to such projects from the state budget and some CZK 100 million (US$ 3 m) from the budget of Czech Railways. By the year 2007, the development of the railway infrastructure is expected to cost some CZK 85 billion (US$ 3.1 bn) from the state budget. Other funds will be acquired by way of loans.

Waterway infrastructure

Currently, goods and passenger transport in the Czech Republic make intensive use of the Elbe-Moldau route. Measuring 303 kilometres in total, this waterway is linked to West European waterways via the Elbe. Due to the division of the ČSFR the Czech Republic lost direct connections to the Danube. Consequently, the possibility of making the lower Moravia River navigable is being considered.

The Elbe is currently navigable up to Chvaletice. Most of the Elbe-Moldau route meets Class IV standards and the section between Mělník and the state frontier with Germany meets Class Va standards of the International Classification, while limiting vessel width to 10.5 metres. There are nine public ports, of which Děčín, Ústí nad Labem, Mělník and Prague can provide container handling.

In 1995, waterway transport carried a total of 4.43 million metric tons of goods in the Czech Republic, including 1.66 million metric tons internationally.

In the future, the main tasks concerning the development of water-ways infrastructure include making the Elbe navigable as far as Pardubice, building a central port in Pardubice to serve East Bohemia and Moravia, improvement of the navigation conditions in the border sector of the Elbe, and modernisation of existing ports.

Air transport infrastructure

Air transport is currently the most rapidly developing form of trans-portation in the Czech Republic. International passenger air travel grew by 69 per cent in the years 1992–1994, up to 2.9 million passengers a year. Prague-Ruzyně airport holds the dominating position, carrying 95 per cent of all international flights. To meet this expanded demand, the Prague-Ruzyně is undergoing a massive expansion.

The optimum capacity of the existing airport is 2.3 million passengers a year. This capacity however, has been constantly exceeded by about one-third. This year's projections foresee 3.6 million passengers using the facility. The goal of the reconstruction project in the year 1997 is to allow a capacity of 4.8 million passengers a year under conditions comparable to European standards. The construction of a new terminal is funded from a state-guaranteed loan. Upgrading of the runway system, including new equipment, is under preparation. These improve-ments will allow aircraft operation down to runway visibility of 50 metres (aircraft operation is currently limited down to 400 metres visibility). These improvements will allow the airport to reach the projected capacity of 10 million passengers per year.

The privatisation and development of other airports, such as Karlovy Vary, Ostrava-Mošnov, and Brno-Tuřany, are also under inten-sive preparation. Air traffic is to be extended also to some former military airfields.

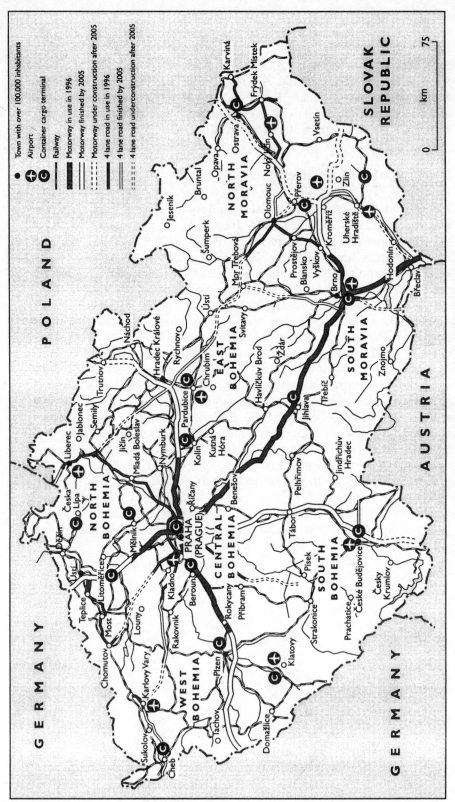

THE TRANSPORT INFRASTRUCTURE

Town with over 100,000 inhabitants
Airport
Container cargo terminal
Railway
Motorway in use in 1996
Motorway finished by 2005
Motorway under construction after 2005
4 lane road in use in 1996
4 lane road finished by 2005
4 lane road underconstruction after 2005

0   km   75

GERMANY

POLAND

SLOVAK REPUBLIC

AUSTRIA

GERMANY

NORTH MORAVIA

SOUTH MORAVIA

EAST BOHEMIA

CENTRAL BOHEMIA

SOUTH BOHEMIA

NORTH BOHEMIA

WEST BOHEMIA

Karviná
Frýdek Místek
Ostrava
Nový Jičín
Vsetín
Opava
Bruntál
Přerov
Zlín
Olomouc
Jeseník
Šumperk
Mor. Třebová
Prostějov
Uherské Hradiště
Kroměříž
Blansko
Vyškov
Hodonín
Brno
Břeclav
Znojmo
Třebíč
Žďár
Svitavy
Jihlava
Havlíčkův Brod
Ústí
Náchod
Hradec Králové
Rychnovo
Chrudim
Pardubice
Jičín
Semily
Trutnov
Liberec
Jablonec
Kolín
Kutná Hora
Nymburk
Mladá Boleslav
Benešov
Pelhřimov
Jindřichův Hradec
Tábor
Písek
Čeština
Děčín
Ústí
Teplice
Litoměřice
Mělník
Most
Chomutov
Louny
Rakovník
Kladno
Beroun
PRAHA (PRAGUE)
Říčany
Rokycany
Příbram
Strakonice
České Budějovice
Český Krumlov
Prachatice
Klatovy
Domažlice
Tachov
Plzeň
Karlovy Vary
Sokolov
Cheb

30

Customs Matters

*Eurotariff**

The Czech Republic was a founder member of the GATT (the predecessor to the present World Trade Organisation) and is a member of the World Customs Organisation. The Czech Customs Law of 1993 brought its procedures very much into line with EU legislation – the Czechs use the harmonised system. Export tariffs are not levied and import levies, which until the end of 1994 were part of the charges imposed on some imported agricultural commodities, were substantially reduced following the Uruguay Round. In view of the minimal use of non-tariff barriers to trade, the import and export regime of the Czech Republic is very liberal and transparent.

Under the Association Agreement, relations between the EU and Czech customs authorities are becoming closer. There are regular meetings between officials to help resolve bilateral difficulties. Phare funds have been channelled to the Czech authorities for the modernisation of Czech customs procedures, laboratory and testing equipment, computerisation under both the national multi-annual Phare programme and multi-country programme. Experts including legal specialists have been seconded to the Czech customs to help prepare new customs legislation covering drug enforcement and smuggling.

With few exceptions, mainly South Pacific Islands, the Most Favoured Nation (MFN) rates of duty apply to imports. Average MFN rates are shown in Table 30.1.

Table 30.1 Average MFN rates of duty

MFN average rates of duty (%)	Global	Agricultural products	Other
Before Uruguay Round	5.89	13.05	5.25
After Uruguay Round	4.54	9.34	4.10

Source: Czech Customs Authorities

---

* Eurotariff operates as a division of Cerrex Ltd

The tariff reductions agreed under the Uruguay Round are to continue for a number of years, mainly until 1999 for most industrial products but longer for agricultural products and sensitive products including textiles, chemicals and pharmaceuticals.

Trade preferences

Preferential rates are applied to more than 50 per cent of the total volume of imported products.

European Union

Most industrial products imported into the EU from the Czech Republic are duty free.

EU exports to the Czech Republic benefit from reducing duties, with duty free access to be achieved by the year 2001 depending on the product group category. Some sensitive products continue to be more restricted – some agricultural products, for example, face a mixture of high duties, quotas and ceilings under which imports into the Czech Republic from the EU enter at a reduced rate, and textiles and steel face a mixture of quotas and double monitoring arrangements. After 1997 non-tariff protection is expected to continue only on a limited range of agricultural products.

Table 30.2 Imports into the Czech Republic from the EU – Industrial Products – reductions on the MFN rate

	Jan 1993	Jan 1995	Jan 1996	Jan 1997	Jan 1998	Jan 1999	Jan 2000	Jan 2001
Product Group A	duty free							
Group B (%)		34	69	100				
Group C (%)		10	25	40	55	70	80	100

Central European free trade area

The Central European Free Trade Agreement between the Czech Republic, Republic of Hungary, Poland and Slovak Republic, Slovenia (with possibly other Central European countries and the Baltics to be added) was signed on 21 December 1992 with the prime objective of the creation of an industrial duty free area by 2001. Slovenia joined later, and there are possibilities that other Central and Eastern European countries and the Baltics will join shortly.

The trade agreements have seven Protocols. Protocols one to three deal with industrial products and Protocols four to six with agriculture (HS Ch 1–24) and the seventh with origin rules. Protocol four covers trade between the Czech Republic/Slovakia and Hungary; Protocol five covers trade between the Czech Republic/Slovakia and Poland; Protocol six covers trade between Hungary and Poland. Each of these Protocols has five Annexes which give the products listed varying degrees of duty preference. Where products are not on any Annex, they do not benefit from any duty preference.

Slovakia

In addition there exists also a customs union in the Slovak Republic, by which goods of Czech origin enter Slovakia duty free and vice versa – at present VATs are at different levels. Licence regulations, customs formalities and other regulations relating to the import, export and transshipment of goods are also unified within the customs union.

Others

Free Trade Agreements exist between the Czech Republic and Slovenia (since 1 January 1994) and Romania (since 1 January 1995) and the EFTA states – the latter very similar to the EU agreement covering industrial products and agricultural goods. Agreement with Lithuania, Turkey and Israel is expected to be in force at the end of 1996.

Future changes

All the trade agreements should be seen within the context of plans to develop a free trade area covering Western Europe, EFTA, Central Europe and the Baltics by the year 2001, and in the longer term to extend these to cover North Africa and a number of Mediterranean Arab states under the Euro Mediterranean Dialogue. One of the major changes will be in the rules of origin which envisage 'pan-European cumulation'. Pan-European cumulation is due to come into force on 1 January 1997, so that value added in any of the blocs including EU, EFTA, the CEE, the Baltics and some of the former parts of Yugoslavia would count towards origin for duty purposes anywhere within the area, although some countries may have a derogation.

Generalised System of Preferences (GSP)

Import duty preferences are granted to imports originating in developing countries. Imports from the Least Developed Countries are subject to zero duty: others enter at a preferential rate of half the normal duty while for some sensitive products, eg in the textiles sector, no such preferences are granted.

The Czech Republic itself receives such treatment on its exports, for example, Czech exports to the US, Canada, Japan, Australia and New Zealand. To benefit from these the products must be accompanied by the standard Form A certificate, usually confirmed by the Customs and Certification department of the Economic Chamber (Czech Chamber of Commerce).

Duty reliefs

Inward processing relief in respect of materials, components and sub-assemblies imported for processing and export to Europe is in force.

Goods intended for processing completion or final assembly can be imported duty free provided they are to be used for the manufacture of products for export and providing the value of the product to be exported exceeds the customs value for the imported product. Only companies having a foreign capital share of at least 30 per cent, and if this share is not less than CZK 50 million, can benefit. The imported products do not need to be manufactured by the foreign partner in a joint venture, but the imports and compensational exports must go through the foreign partner. At present, new joint ventures can import goods duty free without having to compensate with exports for one year of the date of establishment. Joint ventures established earlier can import duty free for one year from the date on which the decree became valid. The decree is due for review on 31 December 1996, and whether it will be continued, even in a different form, after that date, is uncertain. The Czech Republic has 11 duty free zones, some only within specific companies, and there are no plans at present to introduce more zones. Recent requests to open such zones have been rejected.

Part 4

Building an Organisation

31

Strategic Investment

John Waugh, PA Consulting Group

- We want to make a strategic investment. We need you to identify a suitable target for us.

- We've bought into this Czech company and we are looking for another strategic investment.

- We own a stake in this Czech company and are considering a strategic investment within it.

- We're losing market, losing money and want to know how to develop the business to compete, survive and grow – can you help?

So what's the common denominator – if any?
If one wanted to be unkind, you could say 'Lack of a clear strategy!'
However, this would be too simplistic. These are questions which many of us as advisors have faced on many occasions, not just here in the Czech Republic. What we *do* need to understand is the strategy under-lying these questions, if there is one, in order to provide sensible answers. If no strategy exists or what is there is inadequate then there is an obvious opportunity for us as advisors to provide substantive, value-adding help.

Groan! Not another consultant looking for some poor fellow's watch to tell him the time by and charge enormous amounts for!! Well, that's for the reader, be he British businessman fresh on Czech soil or exist-ing client, to judge.

The purpose of this chapter is to provide an insight into the issues you are likely to face in developing answers to these questions and to outline an approach which has found *practical* application in the Czech market. By that I mean, *results through successful implementation.* Whether it has a value for you remains open.

The last of the questions above was asked by one of my Czech clients, came first chronologically amongst those listed and gave rise to the use of the approach described below.

If you are already here, why are you here? If not, then why do you want to think about coming here?

The answers to these questions provide the starting point for the development of a new strategy for investment which, if managed effectively, will provide rapid and substantive returns.

Your answers need to be clear and quantifiable in *real* business terms. If here already, what were the strategic objectives you laid out originally and how well have they been met? How did you specify those objectives in terms of strategic purpose, financial investment, resource commitment, timescales for achievement, position developed, etc? How were your objectives met in those measures? Is this a sound basis for moving into further investment?

Similarly for the new entrant, the questions become:

- What objectives do you wish to achieve by entering this market?

- How have you set the measures for success with each of the objectives?

- How do these measures compare with 'business as normal', and if different, why?

- What commitments do you plan to make in terms of finance, resources – particularly senior management time and effort – to ensure success?

- What timescales do you intend to operate to?

- What impact failure?

- Who is/are the ultimate decision maker(s) at Board level?

- Why not go to Inverness, have you explored that opportunity? They speak the same language (well, possibly!).

While the list can go on indefinitely, the important issue in both sets of questions is the way in which the objectives can be described, quantified and measured in real business terms – *your* business terms.

Having achieved realistic and quantifiable answers to these and the host of other questions to be asked, the questions of how to make which strategic investment, where and when, and how to manage it, can then be addressed. It is at this point that the development of a new strategy for the business can progress.

Developing a new strategy is time and energy consumptive for the senior management team and will benefit from external stimulii

Whichever the driver, there are attractive opportunities for doing business with a Czech enterprise to generate competitive advantage. Additionally, for the existing investor, there are attractive opportunities in the development and implementation of a new strategy within your current Czech enterprise. Any opportunity will carry with it the need for some degree of strategic investment both within the UK entity and, most certainly, the target Czech business.

The key issue to be tackled in the vast majority of Czech enterprises is that of 'customer focus' – or rather, lack of it. The investment in any enterprise to achieve strategic goals must be customer focus driven if it is going to succeed. However, this is not the only focus to be developed within the top team. They must also have clear sight of the stakeholders requirements and what signifies excellence in the way their business must perform to compete, survive and prosper.

These were the elements brought together in an approach to strategy development and implementation used to good effect in a number of Czech enterprises I have been fortunate enough to work with. This approach is outlined below.

The process does work, much to the benefit of the top management team and the business. Despite the misgivings experienced at the outset, the top teams involved all grew to realise that only they and they alone could own the process. Also, they all admitted that they could not and would not have undertaken the tasks involved, or the activity as a whole, without external support. Without exception, they also agreed it was the most demanding, time and energy consumptive activity they had ever undertaken. I'd go along with that! It has been for me too!!

A consultant-introduced process that works – what's the catch, and how does this relate to strategic investment?

Well, hard work I'm afraid! It will be over six months, before you start to implement the change programme within the business. That's a lot of senior management time, effort and commitment, locally and in the UK – and you still have to make the changes within the business and make them work. *That's Strategic Investment!*

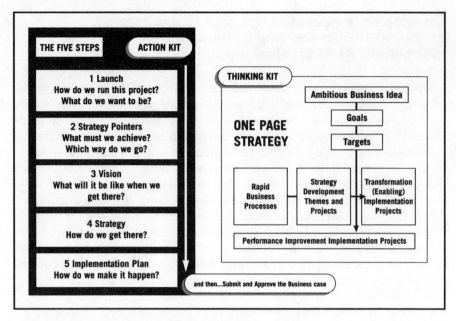

Figure 31.1 The 'One Page Strategy' process

Stage	Main Activities.....leading to.....	Milestone Workshop	Key Decisions	Month	1	2	3	4	5	6
1	Selecting and training the core team. Preparing the top team for the process.	Launch	Project processes, milestone dates. Business ambition; a 'Big Idea'		◗					
2	Developing competitive advantage criteria (external and internal). Goals for clients, stakeholders, excellence. 'What if?' financial modelling.	Strategy Pointers	Ultimate performance goals, targets. Business process bundles, sponsors. Vision development projects, teams. Communications plan.			◗				
	Starting the vision of the future. Coarse modelling of costs and benefits.	*Benefits Scaling*	*Outline vision ideas, sanity check, confirm goals and targets OK.*				○			
3	Designing the future, in detail. How everything will be different More modelling of costs and benefits.	Vision	What it will be like when we get there; why being like that is right. Strategy development projects, teams.					◗		
4	Working out what needs to be done to make it happen. Modelling financial projections.	Strategy	Confirmation of the vision. The full scope of implementation tasks Agreeing the financial implications.						◗	
5	Implementation planning. Refining the financial model. Detailing the resources and timing for change. Preparing for start of implementation.	Implementation Plan	The full implementation plan. Agree the whole One Page Strategy and financial implications. Affirm total, unqualified commitment.							◗
	Preparing the formal Business Case	Business Case	Agree the Business Case Launch implementation.							○

Figure 31.2 The process in outline: 5 stages, 5 (main) milestones
6 months

So, what's the process?

We call it the 'One Page Strategy' process. It's a five-stage process, as illustrated in figure 31.1 This process was first developed and used in the UK nearly ten years ago and has subsequently gained an impressive user community amongst world class companies around the world. It takes time to work through the process, despite what many clients have thought when taking their first steps along the route. Typical milestones are illustrated in figure 31.2.

To guide the management team, we provide a Strategic Thinking Kit (see figure 31.3) and encourage them to formulate their strategic ideas on one sheet. The first step is to get them to develop a mission or ambitious idea for the business. Then they must describe this in terms of three sets of goals, from the point of view of their customers, their stakeholders and their internal performance.

The next step is to identify quantifiable targets with these goals and sets of 'Business Process Bundles' which own the goals (figure 31.4).

The team must decide which top manager will 'sponsor' the development of which Business Process Bundle. This done, the top of the One Page Strategy can be completed (figure 31.5).

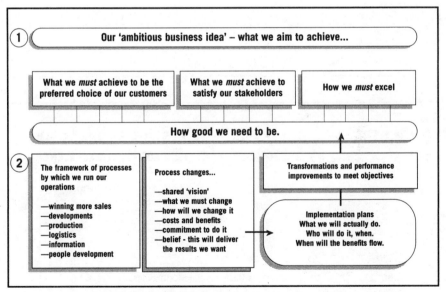

Figure 31.3 A Strategic Thinking Kit (two entry points 1 and 2)

The next task is to develop the vision of how the business will operate in the future and why operating like that will be right. A series of strategy development projects and development teams then need to be selected.

These teams work out what needs to be done to achieve the strategic goals and how to make it happen. This is the *detail strategy development phase* and involves a confirmation of the vision as well as fully scoping the implementation tasks and modelling the financial implications. The result is shown in figure 31.6.

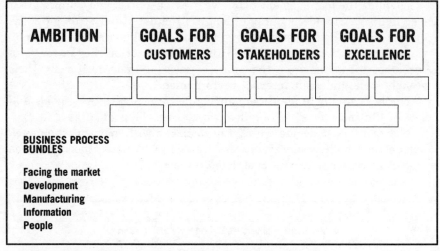

Figure 31.4 'Business Process Bundles' and targets

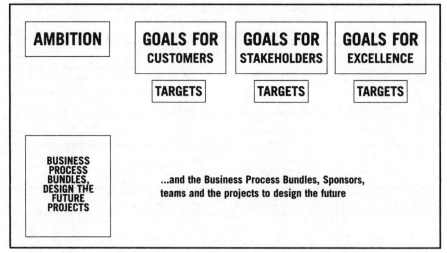

Figure 31.5 Completing the top of the 'One Page Strategy' sheet

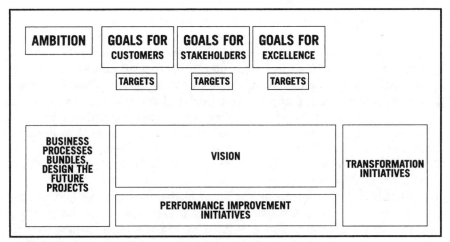

Figure 31.6 Detail strategy development phase

Then comes the hard work of implementation To achieve success there is no substitute for experience with which to guide the management team. Experience of doing things differently and achieving change in the Czech environment, preferably from Czechs who can put 'their hands' on the tiller to show management what to do and how to do it. Remember the following:

● Technical understanding and learning rates are high.

● Productivity is low and management practice weak.

● People are highly resistent to change, mainly because of poor communication, lack of understanding and commitment and weak leadership.

● Investing in people is the primary pre-requisite to restructuring and performance improvement.

When considering making a strategic investment, these points should be remembered. Nothing happens quickly and many companies are scarred by the ebullient claims of western advisors and/or suitors being able to make change successfully, and failing to deliver.

The strategic investment will not be successful unless implementation is realised

From a full description of your strategy and objectives, and a careful selection of your target company, companies or investment projects will face you with your stiffest challenge: how to make it happen!

Even at a simple joint venture level, you will need to consider how best to help your chosen partner to perform to your expectations. Language difficulties aside, your initial encouragement will come in terms of your partner's technical understanding of your technologies. This will be accompanied by an apparent but, in reality, a weak, or non-existent understanding of your managerial philosophy in areas such as quality, purchasing, logistics, performance measures, delivery reliability, etc. Time pressures and personal responsibility to want to perform have not been evident over the last 40 years. Relationships between suppliers and producers have more often been on a proximity or personal friendship rather than a commercial basis.

Reaching further into your initiative, if a joint venture or acquisition is on the cards then a restructuring of the company will have to be faced and planned for. You will have to consider every aspect of the operation, from finance and financial reporting, through culture change and radical surgery into the operational body of the organisation.

Finance systems will need realignment with UK, Euro or GAAP reporting procedures – as well as retaining their ability to satisfy Czech fiscal requirements. Management information, marketing & sales, purchasing & order processing, logistics management, service & support, commercial policies and procedures and quality systems will need to be overhauled, in some cases introduced for the first time.

Firstly people and then processes will need to be addressed. A carefully constructed change management programme, defined by use of the process above, supported by excellent communications and clear objectives will need to be put into place and progressed energetically. This must be seen to deliver business benefit and is a precursor to gaining the commitment to the change you will require. Use of Assessment/Development Centres will help you understand more clearly the potential of your people for personal and team roles and, despite their title, act as clear motivators for the staff involved.

Reengineering of the business processes can then take place more effectively. It is highly likely that the IT systems will need to be redeveloped. Taking a package-enabled (PACE) approach to rapid business change will facilitate this process. Process mapping, gap analysis and process redesign can then be focused on the most productive areas for change. The process redesign can be constrained within the boundaries of the Enterprise Requirement Planning (ERP) system solution rather than drifting freely in a 'no-holds-barred' conceptual environment.

With process reengineering will come the focus for rationalisation and new process introduction. This will spell the start of the restructuring of the business in the visible sense, particularly the physical asset base, whether it occurs across a single or multi-site enterprise. Typically, facilities will need reengineering, if not wholescale reconstruction, mixed with new build – whether in the office or on the factory floor. New processes – particularly customer-oriented – will help to dictate the physical reconstruction as well as to support the reengineered processes. This is equally true for manufacturing industry, the service industry and the utilities.

However, none of this will succeed without the full commitment of the people involved. Their constant motivation, at all levels will be paramount. So far, many companies moving into the Czech Republic have not fully addressed the people issues. Whilst their efforts have focused on and reaped reward from the physical restructuring to a degree, the commitment needed for longer term competitiveness is still missing.

Everyone entering this market in search of opportunities has faced the issues outlined above. The vast majority all now recognise that human factors, and their effective management in any strategic investment, are key to success. This is true inside the business, as well as outside! Getting this right enables the reengineering of processes, implementation of systems and rationalisation of the business to happen more quickly and more smoothly, and the investment to pay dividends.

32

Investment Finance

Christian Kaltenegger, Creditanstalt

The overall investment needs of the Czech economy are substantial. Transformation is not only about changing from a centrally planned to a market economy, though this is very important, it is also about changing the minds of the people – and very substantially – about altering the quality of fixed investment. However, these high investment needs – real fixed capital investment increased by about 16 per cent in 1995 and is expected to rise substantially within coming years – are experienced in an environment with low domestic capital formation in the household sector, rather strained cash flow conditions in the enterprise sector and a troubled banking system with limited ability to efficiently fulfil its functions of resource allocation and term transformation. Overall, domestic sources for investment finance are rather scarce and not too attractive – at least for foreign investors and at this moment in time. This is why foreign banks still play a significant role in servicing foreign companies in the Czech Republic.

Interest rates

Interest rates in the Czech Republic are still high, with the three-month PRIBOR (Prague Inter-Bank Offered Rate) eight percentage points above the three-month FIBOR (Frankfurt Inter-Bank Offered Rate) in deutschmarks. This is due mainly to the comparatively high Czech inflation rate and the rather restrictive monetary policy imposed by the Czech National Bank (CNB). In addition, the banking system is loaded with poor quality loans; classified credits make up more than one-third of the aggregate credit portfolio. This forces the banks to keep margins high in order to make the necessary provisions for bad debts. Generally, the banking system still lacks efficiency, with the number of banks and employees still expanding. The three major banks still dominate the credit market, with a combined market share of about 60 per cent in 1994, with Komercni Banka alone accounting for 30 per cent of this market.

On the other hand, competition for prime domestic and foreign clients is rather fierce, especially from foreign banks, which explicitly target this group. This forces margins in this business segment down to international standards. However, during the past two years the CNB has been very cautious in granting licences to foreign banks. Domestic companies are much less interesting targets still having to pay average margins of more than two percentage points above PRIBOR. Many of them are having difficulties obtaining finance at all. While this might be understandable from the point of view of the individual banks, it puts a strain on the Czech economy in terms of raising sufficient finance to support fixed investment.

Borrowing

It is becoming increasingly popular for Czech-based enterprises to borrow in foreign currency since the exchange rate is stable and foreign interest rates are well below domestic levels. This gives foreign banks a competitive edge over many of their Czech competitors. In fact, the former have expanded their foreign currency lending, thereby pushing up their foreign currency liabilities to about 50 per cent of those of the whole banking system, while their share in total outstanding credits accounts only for eight per cent.

Overall, the offer of banking services has improved significantly over the past few years with a wide range of payment services, electronic banking and corporate banking now available. The product range in working capital loans is already quite comprehensive and includes overdraft facilities, term loans and advances both in CZK and foreign currency. Investment finance offering terms of up to ten years is also available. However, banks are still very cautious with regard to the maturity structure of their loan portfolio: only about 30 per cent is accounted for by credits with a maturity of over four years, another 30 per cent represents medium-term maturities, which leaves 40 per cent of the total as short-term finance with a term of less than one year. The pattern is even more accentuated with newly granted short-term credits: these account for more than three-quarters of total new credit.

The most common types of collateral are mortgages, guarantees and assignments of claims. Project finance is available, provided the borrower holds a substantial share in the equity of the project and submits a comprehensive feasibility study. Since housing and property development is expected to form a substantial business segment over the next decade, mortgage banking, which began to emerge only recently, will play an important role in meeting the financing needs of these businesses.

With the Czech banking system being troubled in some areas, the capital market should also play an important role in financing the huge investment needs of the Czech economy. Major Czech companies tap the bond market in order to raise finance. However, as long as foreign credit is comparatively more attractive than any domestic source of finance, the domestic market will stay rather thin.

Investment programmes

Even though the government refrains mostly from interventions in the economy, it has launched five different programmes to promote investment:

- **START** provides interest subsidies for credit amounts of up to CZK 10 million for small businesses (companies with up to 24 employees) in order to finance projects that create new employment, enhance technological or ecological quality, stimulate exports or relate to information and consulting services.

- **ZARUK** targets companies with up to 500 employees and provides guarantees for credit denominated in domestic currency.

- **ROZVOJ** helps companies with up to 500 employees in problem regions by granting an interest rate subsidy.

- **REGION** requires participation in START or ROZVOJ and provides an extra interest rate subsidy for companies in problem regions.

- Finally, **SPECIAL** also requires participation in **ZARUK**, **START** or **ROZVOJ**. It grants an extra monthly subsidy of CZK 1000 for every job created by a new project.

As already mentioned, combinations of the different programmes are possible, but the overall subsidy must not exceed the total annual interest payment. Only one project per applicant and per year can be filed and subsidies are limited to projects realised in the Czech Republic. Applications have to be filed through Ceskomoravska Zarucni a Rozvojova Banka (CMZRB), a guarantee and development bank. Application forms are available from most banks.

Even though quite a few fundamental problems remain, the overall structure of investment finance in the Czech Republic is gradually improving. Long-term finance is already available, the capital market for debt and equity is becoming more liquid, the service level of the banking system is converging towards western standards and the margins, though still high, are decreasing.

33

Foreign Investment

Dr Irena Edwards and Petr Zeman,
McKenna & Co

Since 1989 the government has introduced specific policies which have had a positive effect on the investment climate in the Czech Republic. The country has been quick to establish itself as an open market, receptive to foreign investment. Commercial legislation has been introduced to provide foreign investors with equal rights and obligations to those of their Czech counterparts. The Commercial Code of 1991 repealed 84 laws previously designed to make foreign investment very difficult, including the Act on Economic Relations with Foreign Countries and the Act on Enterprises with Foreign Capital Participation. Under the Commercial Code foreigners may conduct business in the Czech Republic under the same conditions and to the same extent as a Czech national. Unlike some other former socialist countries, official authorisation is not normally required for the foundation of a company. Legislation has also been introduced to provide investor protection, while in 1995 the long-awaited Foreign Exchange Act was passed, providing for the convertibility of the Czech crown on the current account of the trade balance.

Opportunities for the investor

There has been a dramatic shift away from the pre-1989 joint venture law which initially prevented foreign parties from holding a majority interest in Czech companies and subsequently insisted on at least a token Czech shareholding. Now a foreign investor may invest in the Czech Republic by establishing an enterprise with 100 per cent participation of foreign capital, by entering into a joint venture with a Czech entrepreneur or by investing in an existing enterprise.

A new or existing enterprise may assume the form of a joint-stock company, a limited liability company, a general commercial partnership, a limited partnership or a cooperative. Foreign investors often find the joint-stock company and the private company limited by shares the most practical and appropriate business form.

In the vast majority of instances official approval from the Ministry of Finance is no longer required for the establishment of a joint venture. Only if the Czech party is a state enterprise will the joint venture require specific government approval, while in some strategic fields such as banking, insurance and mining it is necessary to obtain a licence. However, this requirement applies equally to foreign and domestic entrepreneurs.

Foreign investors are generally at liberty to buy shares in Czech-owned companies. Indeed, the success of the Czech Republic privatisation process has offered many opportunities for foreign investors who have committed their capital and know-how to privatised joint-stock companies. As the opportunities to become involved in the privatisation process are coming to an end, foreign investors are looking at indirect investments in standard capital markets such as The Prague Stock Exchange which reopened in April 1993 and has developed in competition with the second exchange known as the RM System which deals in securities by way of a continuous auction. Non-residents are still prohibited from buying real estate, a problem which can nevertheless be overcome by establishing a Czech company to hold the property or by leasing property. Significantly the law on valuation of land and buildings has removed the distinction between fully domestic companies and those with foreign capital participation, in so far as land prices are concerned. Previously when foreign-owned Czech companies purchased land, the price for land tax purposes was calculated on the basis of world market prices, which meant those applicable in Germany and Austria. Now the same regime applies to all companies.

Investor protection

A key aspect in maintaining investor confidence is ensuring protection for the investment. Generally investments are protected against expropriation by the Constitution while the Czech Republic has entered into bilateral investment protection agreements with most of the EC member countries, the US and other countries. Expropriation may be accomplished and ownership rights curtailed only in compliance with the relevant laws and only with the payment of compensation. Compensation paid to a foreign investor in these circumstances will be freely transferable abroad and can be converted into the foreign currency in which the foreign partner contributed the initial capital for the enterprise.

In addition to bilateral agreements for the promotion and protection of investments the Czech Republic is also a party to numerous bilateral double taxation agreements. Thus dividends paid to a British shareholder which are normally subject to 25 per cent withholding tax are only subject to a tax rate of 5 per cent if the foreign recipient controls 25 per cent of the business, or 15 per cent if it controls less than 25 per cent.

Foreign Exchange Act

The passing of the long-awaited Foreign Exchange Act which came into effect on 1 October, 1995 has brought important changes for investors. The Act represented a milestone in the transformation of the Czech economy because it provided for the convertibility of the Czech crown on the current account of the trade balance pursuant to Article 8 of the IMF Treaty, opening the door for the Czech Republic to join OECD, which it did at the end of 1995. In addition to the positive effects on the Czech economy, the Act also has important benefits for foreign investors.

In relation to foreign exchange non-residents (which includes sole traders and branch offices based in the Czech Republic), the Act now enables them to convert their Czech crown income to any hard currency freely. This has effectively removed the disadvantage of a branch office requiring a Czech National Bank (CNB) licence to use local Czech crown income to meet foreign currency payments.

Regarding foreign exchange residents, the Act has made two significant changes in relation to access to foreign currency and investments abroad. The Act removes the obligation on foreign exchange residents to offer their foreign currency to local banks and the ability to open foreign exchange accounts in the Czech Republic without the need for a CNB licence. In addition foreign exchange residents are allowed to make financial or other undertakings to non-residents. The Act consists of several mechanisms to assist in monitoring and regulating the flow of foreign exchange, including a duty on foreign exchange residents to notify the appropriate state authorities of financial credits towards foreign exchange non-residents, direct and indirect investments abroad as well as notification of accounts abroad.

Conclusion

There exists a positive framework for foreign investment in the Czech Republic. In the aftermath of the velvet revolution of 1989 a principle of equity was adopted at an early stage between the foreign investor and the domestic one. Initially this was reflected by the significant opportunities to invest in all the privatisation schemes (with the exception of voucher privatisation and employee stock). Subsequent foreign investment has been directed towards other opportunities including the stock exchange and joint stock companies. The Czech government has introduced a number of measures to guarantee investor protection, thereby maintaining confidence in this developing market. The only significant restriction on investor freedom is the opportunity to invest in property, a problem which can be overcome. Finally the Foreign Exchange Act of 1995 should help to ensure the continued attraction of the Czech Republic as a place for foreign investment.

34

Setting up a Company

*Dr Irena Edwards and Ian Parker,
McKenna & Co*

Foreign companies wishing to conduct business in the Czech Republic usually set up a subsidiary company or a branch office there. Setting up a company can take some time and the consequent advantage of a branch office is that it is a simpler and quicker way of establishing a business presence in the Czech Republic.

Whether a branch office is chosen rather than a company will not depend solely on speed. For example a branch office does not constitute a Czech legal entity and is instead regarded as a foreign entity; foreign entities cannot own land in the Czech Republic. Also any liability attaching to the branch office will automatically attach to the company of which it is a branch. On the other hand a branch office may have accounting and tax advantages, particularly if the branch is to conduct a great deal of business on behalf of the company to which it is attached.

This chapter deals with the formation of 'limited liability companies' (abbreviated in Czech as 's.r.o.') and joint-stock companies (abbreviated in Czech as 'a.s.'), although much of the procedure described below is also applicable to the setting up of a branch. For example a branch office, like a company, must obtain a trade licence, a lease of premises and be registered on the Commercial Register.

The S.R.O.

This type of company is the most common legal form for small and medium-sized businesses and for subsidiaries of foreign parents. It is similar to the UK private limited company, but is not so versatile. The company does not issue shares, but each member holds an 'ownership interest' which is calculated as the proportion which the member's contribution bears to the company's total registered capital. The minimum capital requirement is 100,000 Czech Crowns (CZK) and the minimum amount for any one member's contribution is 20,000 Czech Crowns.

Because the company does not issue shares, it is more difficult to transfer and restructure ownership interests than in a UK private limited company, where shares can be transferred and issued relatively simply. If it is envisaged that the ownership interests in the company will be changing (for example in order to bring in investors) then the a.s. (see below) will be a more appropriate vehicle.

An s.r.o. can have a sole member. The maximum number of members of an s.r.o. is 50.

The A.S.

This type of company corresponds to the UK plc and is more heavily regulated than the s.r.o. Its ownership is established by the issue of shares. For some businesses this legal form is a requirement of law, for instance in the case of banks and pension or investment funds. The minimum registered capital is one million Czech Crowns (CZK). An a.s. can be founded by a sole shareholder, which cannot, however, be a native person.

Formation

Dormant companies are not officially recognised in the Czech Republic. A company which is not trading will still have the same filing and administrative requirements as an actively trading company. This fact and the minimum share capital requirements set out above mean that off-the-shelf companies do not exist in the Czech Republic. All companies must be tailor-made.

The company comes into existence on registration at the Commercial Register. The process of registration is conducted through application to a court. To make an application a series of documents must be submitted (see below). The exact length of time the formation of the company will take will depend on a number of factors, in particular the extent of local contacts. For example if a Czech national is to be a director of the company, this will eliminate the considerable time taken to obtain a residence permit for a foreign director. Even when all the documents have been submitted to the court, actual registration can take a number of months, and if the court is dissatisfied with any particular document this can lead to considerable delay.

The following documents will need to be submitted in order to obtain registration:

1   documents evidencing the existence of the parent company (such as the certificate of incorporation);

2 a power of attorney authorising a person to sign incorporation documentation and to act on behalf of the parent company in establishing the Czech company;

3 incorporation documentation;

4 specimen signatures of directors;

5 evidence of payment of capital;

6 residence permits (for foreign directors);

7 a statement of trustworthiness signed by each director and each member of the supervisory board (a supervisory board, which plays an oversight role, is mandatory in the case of an a.s.);

8 extracts from the criminal register in respect of proposed directors and members of the supervisory board;

9 business licences;

10 a petition to the court for registration of the company.

A number of the above documents will be required to be signed in front of a notary public (if signed in the UK the document will need to be superlegalised at the Czech Embassy in London), and all documents not in the Czech language will have to be accompanied by a Czech translation stamped by a court-appointed translator.

In order to speed up the process, it is essential that the person or entity establishing the company devotes time and attention as soon as possible to the following three issues: obtaining a lease, obtaining a business licence and obtaining residence permits.

Lease

In order to obtain the business licence referred to below, a lease or licence must be entered into in respect of premises and signed in front of a notary public. This must be obtained in order to allow the new company to have a registered office in the Czech Republic. It is very important to ensure that the lease is for a property in which the type of activity contemplated for the company is permitted. For example a purely residential lease will not be sufficient for a business licence to be obtained.

Business licence

For most business activities it is necessary to obtain a business licence, which authorises the company to carry out its business activities. The business activities of the company must also be set out in the company's Memorandum of Association or Articles of Association. A company must appoint a physical person whose name will appear on the licence as the authorised representative of the company. The representative must be either a Czech national, or a person with a long-term residence permit who has an adequate level of knowledge of the Czech language. The representative need not be a director of the company, but plays a liaison role between the company and the trade licensing authorities.

Business licences are obtained from the trade licensing office relevant to the area where the company has its registered office. There are two categories of business: notifiable and licensed. The 'notifiable' category is further subdivided into 'free' and 'regulated' trades. The 'free' category includes, for example, the sale and purchase of goods and does not require any particular qualifications. Regulated trades tend to include most skilled trades, while licensed businesses include manufacturing, services and some commercial trades. For regulated and licensed trades certain professional qualifications are usually required. The verification of a foreigner's qualifications can be particularly time consuming and, if possible, the appointment of a Czech national as the representative of the company for the purpose of obtaining the business licence may be a more favourable option as Czechs do not need to obtain a residence permit and verification of qualifications is more straightforward.

Residence permit

The Commercial Register sets out who is authorised to sign on behalf of the company. It is very common in the Czech Republic for parties to contracts to obtain an extract from the Commercial Register to verify who is so authorised. If the appropriate signature is obtained on the contract then the company will be legally bound. Although it is not essential for all proposed directors to have residence permits when the application for registration of the company on the Commercial Register is submitted, the only directors who will appear in the Commercial Register as authorised to sign documents on behalf of the company will be those with residence permits or those who are Czech citizens. Therefore if a foreign owner wishes to keep business control of the company, it is essential that a residence permit be obtained for the foreign director or directors. A foreigner does not have to be resident in the Czech Republic for any minimum period per year in order to obtain a residence permit.

Depending on the exact relationship between the parent company and the foreign director of the subsidiary, the foreign director may also have to obtain a work permit prior to obtaining the residence permit.

Once the company has been registered on the Commercial Register, but not before, it can commence trading. Within 30 days of registration the company will have to register for tax purposes at the local revenue office.

35

Accounting

Martin Levey, Lubbock Fine sro

The former Soviet style regime implemented a rigid accounting system to record the transactions of industrial and commercial enterprises. Although based on double entry bookkeeping, the system was aimed at measuring performance in terms of long-term planning objectives rather than recording or recognising commercial results. This, combined with strong Teutonic influences, has led to an extremely inflexible accounting philosophy where the formal content of transactions takes precedence over their substance and any variation or interpretation is automatically presumed in contravention with the strict regulations.

In 1992 a far-reaching reform of the accounting system was introduced which was designed to be more compatible with International GAAP and generally follow the European Union's fourth and seventh directives. Having said that, anyone taking a quick glance at a set of Czech accounts will (notwithstanding the language) immediately notice an unfamiliar layout which does not lend itself to easy interpretation.

The main reforms introduced in 1992 differentiated, for the first time, accounting policies adopted for financial statements from the taxing regulations. Financial statements are to assume concepts of prudence and in particular show current assets at the lower of cost or net realisable value. Enterprises can use commercially based depreciation policies. Substantial groups of companies must prepare and publish consolidated statements.

Almost five years after these reforms there is still a general misconception that the tax return shows the real results while the financial statements, if different, show...well, something else! There is a reluctance (perhaps brought on by lack of experience – perhaps for other reasons) in providing for bad or doubtful debts on a commercial – rather than a taxation – basis. Consolidated financial statements are rarely seen and Annual Reports are often incomplete, inaccurate, and considered privileged information, available only on a 'need to know' basis.

Companies listed on the various stock and over the counter markets still make premature announcements of their results which are then subject to wild fluctuations during the course of the annual audit.

Notwithstanding the difficulties in reliably assessing current performance, directors regularly announce future profits with impunity.

In short, although there is a highly developed system of accounting,
this still fails to produce reliable information on which to make
commercial or investment decisions. It is only the foolhardy who do not
carry out due diligence and check all accounting information – no matter
how large or small the enterprise with whom they are dealing (or
indeed who its auditors are).

Accounting records

Enterprises registered with the Commercial Courts must keep accounting
records on an accruals basis, using the double entry system prescribed
under Czech regulation. This requires a statutory chart of accounts to
be adopted, classifying entries into the following main categories:

0   Fixed assets
1   Inventory
2   Financial accounts
3   Receivables and payables
4   Capital and long-term liabilities
5   Expenses
6   Revenues

Each category is grouped in accordance with the headings in the
financial statements. Main accounts are identified by a three digit code
stipulated in the regulations, although sub-analytical accounts can be
set up at the discretion of the enterprise.

Czech accounting regulation applies equally to enterprises with
foreign investment. In practical terms this means that Czech accounts
must be maintained in full and any variance with head office format
or accounting policies must be adjusted outside the statutory books as
a separate accounting exercise.

General accounting requirements

Financial Statements are made up to 31 December and are to be
submitted with the annual tax return to the Finance Office for the
district in which the enterprise has its seat, by 31 March following. The
filing deadline can be extended where the enterprise has appointed
a duly qualified tax advisor.

The Financial Statements comprise a balance sheet and profit and
loss account and explanatory notes. These shall include:

- General
  - Details of subsidiaries
  - Details of employees and staff costs
  - Directors' remuneration

- Accounting policies
  - Methods of valuing capitalised assets, inventories and investments
  - Changes in accounting policy
  - Basis of provisions
  - Depreciation methods and rates
  - Foreign currency translation

- Notes to the balance sheet and profit and loss account
  - Analysis of investments
  - Movements in capital and reserves
  - Dividends
  - Market value of assets where significantly different from balance sheet
  - Leased assets
  - Details of overdue receivables and payables
  - Movements in provisions
  - Charges securing receivables and liabilities
  - Contingent liabilities
  - Analysis of income split between domestic and foreign markets.

General accounting policies

- Intangible assets
  Included at cost and amortised over five years. Research and development costs must be separately identifiable and relate to a project which will generate future income.

- Tangible assets
  Included at cost and depreciated at commercial rates. Replacement cost basis is also permissible but rarely used.

- Inventory
  At the lower of cost and net realisable value after making provision for obsolete or slow moving items (not deductible for tax purposes). Physical stocktakes must be undertaken at least once (during the last three months of the year) or stock may be verified and evidenced by a perpetual inventory system. LIFO or replacement cost bases are not permitted.

- Receivables
  At the lower of cost and net realisable value after making provision
  for bad and doutbful debts. (There are special rules for the calculation
  of tax deductible bad debts and these often get substituted when
  making provision for accounting purposes.)

- Bank balances
  Due to the nature of the banking system – which uses transfers
  rather than cheques – bank balances are shown on a cleared item
  basis.

- Balances in foreign currency
  Included at the official exchange rate at the year end. Unrealised
  losses are recognised (although not tax deductible). No credit is
  taken for unrealised gains.

- Leased assets
  With the exception of leased assets which include some element of
  real estate, leasing costs are treated as a revenue expense and are
  not capitalised.

- Extraordinary items
  Includes such items as the effect of a change in accounting or
  valuation policy, adjustment to the valuation of acquired assets and
  – least extraordinary of all – bad debts not recovered after
  bankruptcy proceedings.

- Deferred tax
  Arising from the different calculation of taxable profit and reported
  profit. Currently limited to depreciation adjustments. Not frequently
  seen.

Audit requirements

An annual audit is required for all joint stock (as) companies. Limited
liability companies (sro) need only have an audit where turnover
exceeds CZK 40 million (approximately US$1.5 million) or net assets
exceed CZK 20 million (approximately US$750 000).

Audits are carried out in accordance with the regulations of
the Chamber of Auditors which are closely based on International
Auditing Standards (in theory if not always in practice). The audit
report does not have to be filed with the annual financial statements
at the Finance Office – indeed there appears to be no deadline for
the completion of the audit. This helps to explain why announced

resuilts often differ from audited accounts and why audit qualifications are commonplace.

The audit report is required to be attached to a copy of the financial statements to which it applies.

36

Tax

Martin Levey, Lubbock Fine sro

The Czech Republic has developed into one of the most attractive and stable Central European countries for investment opportunities. The major waves of privatisation are complete and there is a healthy and growing private sector offering many opportunities to develop new business with both foreign and local capital.

In 1993 an overhauled tax system was introduced and this continues to be modified and amended. Apart from the main taxing legislation, separate regulations and explanations are approved and published frequently. There is no separate appeal tribunal against tax rulings, which must be pursued either in separate negotiations with the Ministry of Finance or, failing that, through the civil courts (a lengthy process).

Special concessions no longer exist for businesses with foreign investors which are taxed in much the same way as other Czech entities. As can be expected from a new system operating in such a new economy, there are still major areas of complexity and uncertainty.

The main business taxes are:

- corporate income tax
- personal income tax
- value added tax
- property tax.

Corporate income tax

All corporate entities and permanent establishments operating in the Czech Republic are taxed on their profits as shown in their annual tax return. The tax and accounting year runs to 31 December for all. The rate of corporate income tax has been steadily reducing from the introduction of the new tax system and for 1996 stands at 39 per cent.

Taxable profits are arrived at after deducting expenses incurred to earn or maintain trading income including depreciation of fixed assets at prescribed rates. Non-allowable costs include entertainment

Table 36.1 Czech corporate entities

---

a Foreign branch
A permanent establishment which must be registered with the commercial court. Cannot hold immovable property in its own right.

b General commercial partnership (vos)
Partners have unlimited liability.

c Limited partnership (ks)
Has both general partners and partners whose liability is limited to their investment in the partnership.

d Limited liability company (sro)
Founded by registered members who enjoy limited liability. Minimum capital requirement is CZK100 000 (approximately US$3750)

e Joint stock company (as)
A limited liability company with shares. Minimum capital requirement is CZK1million (approximately US$37 500)

---

expenses, costs of raising capital, costs of penalties and fines and expenses in excess of stipulated limits. Foreign branches can still negotiate a separate basis for taxation.

Withholding tax of 25 per cent is deducted from dividends. There is no overall scheme for relief of double taxes between members of Czech groups of companies, although there is a partial 50 per cent relief against the double taxation of dividends paid to a Czech parent company.

Withholding tax is due on payment abroad of dividends, interest, royalties, leases and in some instances management charges. Losses made in companies subsequent to 1993 can be carried forward for up to five years. Losses incurred after 1 January 1995 are available for seven years.

There are thin capitalisation rules which disallow the deduction of interest paid to related parties where loans exceed four times the registered capital (six times for related banks and insurance companies and ten times for non-related foreign parties). The excess interest may be treated as a distribution and subjected to withholding tax. Thin capitalisation rules do not apply in the year of an entity's formation, nor the following three years.

Exchange controls have been relaxed and most transactions now need only be reported rather than formally approved. There are no real restrictions on the repayment of foreign loans or the repatriation of capital and profits.

Personal income tax

Individuals present in the Czech Republic for a total of 183 days or more in a calendar year are generally subject to Czech tax on their worldwide income. Special concession is given to foreign experts working in the Czech Republic who are only taxed on their Czech source income after a special relief of 25 per cent (this special relief is soon to be withdrawn).

Taxable benefits include the provision of a car for personal use. In certain circumstances living accommodation can be provided free of tax. Deductions include personal allowances and social security costs, medical and unemployment insurance. The current rate of personal income tax rises to 40 per cent on annual taxable income over CZK 564 000 (approximately US$21 000).

In addition to the 183-day test, independent consultants are subject to a 25 per cent withholding tax if they have a base regularly available to them in the Czech Republic. Non-residents are subject to tax on all Czech source income.

Profits arising from the sale of investments in Joint Stock companies held for over three months or limited liability companies held for over five years are tax free. This exemption applies to residents and non-residents alike.

Value added tax and property tax

Taxable entities who carry on a commercial activity in the Czech Republic must register for VAT when their turnover for the preceding three months has exceeded CZK 750 000 (approximately US$28 000). Voluntary registration is also possible.

Permanent establishments who have not incorporated or otherwise registered with the Commercial Court may not register for VAT.

The standard rate of VAT is 22 per cent on the supply and import of most goods. The supply of services generally attracts tax at the lower rate of 5 per cent as do such items as food, newspapers and pharmaceutical products. The purchase, sale and leasing of property and buildings also attracts VAT at 5 per cent.

The VAT system is based on the European model with all its attendant formalities, complexities and injustices. The Czech system if anything is perhaps more rigid than most, especially in the application of penalties.

Foreigners can still only own property in the Czech Republic through a Czech registered entity (which may be wholly foreign owned). Property transfers carried out on a commercial basis attract property transfer tax of 5 per cent payable by the seller.

Tax treaties

The Czech Republic has over 40 treaties in force with other countries to avoid the incidence of double taxation and to assist in the prevention of fiscal evasion. Favoured jurisdictions for inward investment include the Netherlands, UK and Cyprus – although the latter has been somewhat overworked and is viewed with suspicion by the authorities. The choice of international structure for transactions with, and investments in, the Czech Republic can be complex and requires careful consideration.

37

Property and Law

*Dr Irena Edwards and Sanja Vidaic,
McKenna & Co*

Introduction

There are now numerous opportunities for individuals and companies
to invest in and develop property following the transformation of the
Czech Republic from a centralised command economy to a market
economy.

The notion of private ownership of property was re-established after
the collapse of Communism through the government's programme
of restitution and privatisation. At the same time developers have
concentrated on bringing a quality product to the market and this,
combined with a stable economy, has made the Czech Republic suitable
for equity investment in property. Finally the government has
taken positive action to simplify land ownership procedures and make
financing more accessible to the average population.

Despite the emergence of a stable property market there are nevertheless a variety of hurdles which developers and investors must still
overcome.

Ownership rights

Until 1992 there were considerable difficulties in proving good title due
to a very poor system of property registration; title issues were further
complicated by outstanding restitution problems.

Under the restitution scheme the government has attempted to
return property confiscated during the Communist Regime to its former
owners. The Czech Republic has the largest restitution scheme of all
the former socialist countries with the relevant time for the claim
being the date of the Communist takeover on 25 February 1948. While
the deadline for the submission of restitution claims expired in
December 1992 it will take some time to complete the settlement
of these claims. In addition, further claims will need to be resolved

following the amendments to the restitution laws in February 1996 allowing Czech émigrés who were previously prevented from making claims to submit restitution claims. However, this is not expected to reopen the entire issue as the law also provides that land cannot be restituted if it passed into private ownership after September 1993.

There are two types of restitution procedure. *Natural restitution*, involving the return of confiscated land, is preferred wherever possible. However there are provisions for *financial restitution* when, for example, building has taken place on the land after its nationalisation or in cases where the assets no longer exist.

In 1992 and 1993 new laws were introduced for a modern property registration system. Rights over real property include ownership rights, mortgages, encumbrances, options to purchase and other material rights. To be effective these rights must be entered into the Land Register, a lengthy procedure which can take up to three months and create difficulties for potential purchasers. On a practical level a purchaser will therefore require some security to prevent the vendor from selling to a third party before the registration of ownership is effected. Consequently it may be necessary to withhold the purchase price or place it in an escrow account until registration is complete.

Non-residents are currently prevented from purchasing real estate in the Czech Republic. However this prohibition can be avoided by establishing a Czech corporate vehicle, usually a limited liability company or a joint stock company to hold property. This is a more attractive proposition following the law on valuation of land and buildings which came into force in 1994. The distinction between fully domestic companies and those with foreign capital participation has been removed; one of the consequences is that foreign-owned Czech companies are no longer assessed for land tax purposes on the basis of world market prices.

Finally an important step towards the development of a more realistic property market was taken with the introduction of a law on co-ownership of buildings. This law allows persons and legal entities to acquire ownership rights to individual units in buildings currently owned by municipal authorities and building cooperatives.

Building procedures and regulation

Obtaining development approval is both a lengthy and complicated procedure because of the high number of authorities which are involved in the process. Currently the municipal authorities responsible for zoning and planning are particularly concerned with ensuring that new constructions conform to their surrounding, often historically significant, environment. The development of new constructions and the performance of fundamental reconstructions is governed by the Construction Act and the Law on Administrative Proceedings. It is necessary to obtain a planning permit, construction permit and an occupancy (user) permit. Depending upon the location of the development and its extent, different authorities are involved in granting the permits.

Prior to the commencement of the zoning proceedings which form the basis of the planning approval, a developer must submit a number of statements (up to a total of 44) from various government bodies and agencies in relation to hygiene, fire protection, air pollution, telecommunications, utility, suppliers, roads, protection of historical monuments and other similar matters. The planning permit is granted on the basis of whether the planned project conforms to the master plan for the region and the zoning plan. Once the planning permit has been granted it is valid for two years unless a construction permit is applied for.

The construction permit is issued by the construction office of the relevant District Office or, in the case of a development in Prague, by the building department of the Prague Municipal Office. The documents required for these proceedings – usually totalling 19 – are more detailed than in other Western European countries, and the construction office may request further documents. The proceedings are generally shorter than those needed for obtaining planning approval but can still take two to three months. The construction office ascertains whether all documentation is in accordance with regulations and ensures that there is consistency amongst the bodies' decisions.

A building can be used only once an occupancy permit (*kolaudace*) has been issued. The *kolaudace* involves an oral hearing and a physical inspection of the development. The purpose of these proceedings is to examine whether the building was constructed in accordance with the documentation authorised during the construction proceedings and also to ascertain whether the conditions in the planning permission were complied with. The construction authority can require any defects to be remedied, while penalties can be imposed if occupation takes place before the final approval is given.

Financing

The financial sector in the Czech Republic is undergoing continuous reform and development but at the moment developers thinking of investing in the country face difficulties in obtaining and securing finance. Property development has predominantly been debt-financed because it often represents a cheaper form of finance than equity, particularly when combined with favourable tax concessions.

Debt finance in a developing market such as the Czech Republic also reflects the naturally risk-aversive behaviour patterns of equity investors, a point highlighted by the fact that developments in Prague have tended to be on a pre-let basis rather than speculative.

Leasehold mortgages, a common method of debt financing under many legal systems, are a new concept to the Czech Republic and difficult to obtain. Leases are not regarded by lenders as secured interests in land due mainly to problems of enforcement. Under Czech law, a lease interest is a purely contractual arrangement between the parties; they are not registrable instruments in the Land Register. Under the prevailing interpretation of Czech bankruptcy law, lenders under leasehold mortgages are not regarded as 'secured' creditors so that, if a debtor is declared bankrupt, the lender retains no right over the development to satisfy the debt. However, this security of tenure issue can partly be overcome by registering the lease as an 'encumbrance' to the property in the Land Register. Such registration would bind third parties and would provide lenders with greater rights of enforcement.

This element of taking security has proved most problematic in funding development projects in the Czech Republic. However, the new legislation on mortgages has helped to alleviate some of these problems. In July 1995 amendments to a number of laws took effect with the aim of making mortgages more readily available for the average population. The concept of a mortgage for the purchase and development of property has been widened so that it now includes credit secured not only by real property but also by buildings under construction. An authorised bank can now also issue mortgage bonds which are secured by mortgages over constructions as well as real property. These amendments reflect a movement towards a more sophisticated financial market and the growing number of options for the financing of property acquisitions.

Conclusion

When deciding to invest in the Czech property market there are a number of important practical considerations. Firstly, the length of time involved in obtaining all the relevant approvals can be considerable, a fact which is particularly relevant where developers have entered into pre-let agreements with quality tenants, conditional upon approvals being obtained within certain timeframes. Secondly, it is important to work with people 'on the ground' who have a good knowledge of the prevailing local conditions. Finally the costs of obtaining the approvals from the state administrative authorities should not be underestimated by the developers.

38

Employment Law

Dr Irena Edwards and Petr Zeman, McKenna & Co

The detailed and complex Czech employment laws are regulated primarily by the Labour Code while social security and medical insurance matters are governed by a separate set of laws. Employment and social security laws are mandatory and allow little scope for negotiation between the employer and the employee. Indeed they are designed to protect the employees, a situation which is particularly apparent when considering the conditions for the termination of the employment contracts. Under the Labour Code an employment relationship can arise in three different ways, by employment contract, by election or by appointment. By far the most common method of employment is the employment contract.

The employment contract

Essential terms

To be valid under Czech law an employment contract must contain three essential terms. Firstly there must be a definition of the type of work to be performed by the employee. An employer is only entitled to assign an employee to work not referred to in the contract in a very limited number of cases and consequently the definition of the type of work to be performed should be clear, precise and sufficiently flexible to include alternatives or cover several types of activities. Secondly the employment contract must include a reference to the location of the place of work. If required, alternative work places should be specified because a general right of transfer is unenforceable. The final essential term is a reference to the date on which the work is to commence. Generally the employment contract should be in writing and one copy should be given to the employee.

Conditions of employment

Under Czech law only persons who are over 15 years old and have completed mandatory education are eligible for employment. An employment contract may be concluded for either a definite or an indefinite period of time. Unless the contract expressly provides for a definite period of time an indefinite period is implied. The employment contract may include a probationary period of up to three months at the start of the employment, during which time the contract may be terminated without giving a reason or a period of notice.

The employment contract should specify the number of hours per week the employee is required to work. The maximum number of hours per week is 43 although a smaller number may be agreed upon. Employees are entitled to a break of at least 30 minutes after five hours of work while the working week should be organised in such a way as to provide the employee with at least 12 hours of uninterrupted rest between shifts. Under the Labour Code an employer may not demand more than eight hours overtime in any one week from any employee and no more than 130 hours in any one calendar year. However, such a restriction does not apply to employees involved in transportation, communications and energy or 24 hour operations. An employee who performs overtime work is entitled to a premium of 25 per cent on top of usual pay. Compensation in the form of free time may also be agreed between the employer and the employee instead of an additional overtime payment.

The Czech Republic has a minimum wage which is determined by the Government and is at present CZK 2,500 per month. Wages are usually paid in arrears and at the end of the month, and employees are entitled to be paid in cash. Czech employees are entitled to a basic holiday entitlement of three weeks per calendar year rising to four weeks for an employee who has completed 15 years of employment (this need not be with just one company). If all or part of the entitlement cannot be taken during the calendar year, the company is obliged to carry over the entitlement to the next year. An employee may be remunerated for unused vacation if this was due to authorised reasons or as a result of the termination of the employment. An employee who is required to work during his holiday is entitled to a 50 per cent premium in addition to his usual pay.

All employers are obliged under Czech law to make medical insurance and social security contributions on behalf of their employees, amounting in total to 35.25 per cent of the employee's gross salary (26.25 per cent for social security and 9 per cent for health insurance). An employer is not obliged to make such contributions for foreigners employed either directly from abroad or by a branch of a foreign company in the Czech Republic. The employer is also obliged to register its employees with the local social security administration office and to make the employee's health insurance company aware of the employment. Finally, the employer is under a duty to maintain pension-related records in respect of all its employees.

An employer is liable for employment-related accidents suffered by the employee and is under a duty to insure against his liability for accident and occupational illness. Compensation is payable for loss of earnings, pain and suffering, medical costs and material damage. An employee is liable for any damage he or she causes arising from negligent behaviour during the course of employment, up to a maximum amount of three times the employee's average monthly salary.

Termination of employment

An employment contract for an indefinite period of time may be terminated in a variety of ways. The conditions for termination are set out by law, are mandatory and may not be altered in the employment contract.

Firstly the employer and the employee may by mutual agreement terminate the employment contract. This agreement should be in writing, specify the date on which the relationship shall end and at the employee's request state the grounds for the termination.

Secondly, both the employer and the employee may terminate the employment relationship by serving notice in writing on the other party. Generally the termination period is two months commencing on the first day of the calendar month *following* the month in which notice is served and expires on the last day of the next calendar month. This period is increased to three months for termination by reason of redundancy.

While the employee may serve notice for any reason (or even without providing a reason), the employer may only terminate the contract for specific reasons set out by law. These reasons include organisational considerations (eg restructuring and changes in business activities and technology), health reasons if supported by a medical certificate, failure by the employee to fulfil the conditions set by the labour law regulations for the performance of the agreed work, unsatisfactory performance or a serious breach of work discipline (provided the employer has served a written warning within the relevant time period). In certain circumstances the employer must prove that it is not possible to find alternative suitable employment for the employee within the work place or that the employee is unwilling to transfer to different but appropriate work. Where the employee is made redundant for organisational reasons the employer has a duty to assist in finding other suitable work while the employee is also entitled to severance pay.

Finally, the employer and the employee may terminate the employment relationship immediately but only in exceptional circumstances. Immediate termination is only permissible if the employee is imprisoned or guilty of committing an especially gross breach of work discipline. An employee is entitled to terminate the employment relationship without giving notice if, according to medical opinion, it is not possible to continue working without endangering his health and the employer fails to reassign him to suitable alternative work. In such circumstances the employee is entitled to compensation amounting to what would have been his earnings in the notice period had notice been given.

Conclusion

Czech employment law, although revised and amended since 1989, still has strong ties with the pre-Revolution era. While the power and role of the trade unions has been significantly reduced along with the rights of employees to strike, the Labour Code continues to provide considerable protection for Czech employees. During the next couple of years the Labour Code will probably be revised, although it remains to be seen whether it will be made more relevant to the developing Czech market economy.

Part 5

Appendices

Appendix I:

Sources of Grants and Aid

The British Council

The British Council maintains a network of local contacts with official and commercial bodies in the Czech Republic, and runs a variety of programmes aimed at creating a climate favourable to British trade. In addition to educational and cultural events, it seeks to promote British companies through the management of sponsored activities, and to aid British entrepreneurs through the provision of training for the native workforce.

The latter aim is pursued mainly through the Joint Industrial and Commercial Attach-ments Programme (JICAP) which the Projects Unit of the British Council in Prague administers in conjunction with the Know How Fund. JICAP arranges attachments to British firms for Czech senior and middle managers for periods of up to five weeks. These attachments not only benefit the trainees themselves and their Czech employers, but also help British firms to build up their own set of contacts with firms in the Czech Republic.

In addition, the Council administers and finances a wide-ranging exchange programme, supporting visits in either direction by professionals working in its priority areas: agriculture, cultural heritage, economics and management, education, environment, health, information sciences, law, publishing and media, science and technology and social sciences. Funding will be considered for those presenting papers at conferences, participating in summer schools, specialist courses, training seminars etc.

CzechInvest

An agency of the Czech government, and funded jontly with the EU Phare programme, Czech-Invest seeks to encourage foreign investment in the country. Focusing primarily on 'greenfield' and joint venture projects, it targets sectors which increase capital formation and bring benefits to recently privatised industries, eg automobiles, electronics and precision engineering.

CzechInvest offers potential investors a number of free services, designed to facilitate the establishment of foreign firms in the Czech Republic, and can provide:

● accurate investment data, and information on, for example, doing business in the Czech Republic or specific sectors. Extensive market or feasibility studies cannot be financed however;

● assistance with the organisation of visits, and help in dealing with government organisations (with whom it maintains a network of links);

● aid in managing the investment process itself. CzechInvest is divided into four departments, each with its own function:

—the Greenfield Projects division can offer help in the search for an existing facility or a site for new development, in the construction and recruitment phases, and during any subsequent expansion.

—the Joint Ventures section maintains a database of Czech companies interested in foreign cooperation, which can be matched with British firms, and can also offer help in choosing a location and negotiating procedures.

—the Regions department uses CzechInvest's network of eleven local representative offices in the Czech Republic to pinpoint suitable sites and then assist foreign companies with the implementation of investment plans.

—The Marketing and Public Relations department maintains contact with the media, prepares presentations for potential investors, and manages direct marketing programmes.

Department of Trade and Industry (DTI)

The DTI, as well as jointly running the Know How Fund (see later) administers a number of programmes of interest to those wishing to do business with the Czech Republic.

● The Overseas Project Fund, administered by the Projects Export Promotion Division, makes aid available to UK companies pursuing contracts which will lead to a supply of UK goods or services worth more than £50m. Financial help can offset the cost of feasibility studies, consultancy fees etc, the exact amount depending on the content, duration and potential benefits of the project.

● The HOTS (Hands-on Training Scheme for Overseas Decision Makers) helps British firms bring Czechs of actual or potential procurement influence to the UK to learn about western technology, industrial practices and management techniques. In the process, the host company's services and products become better known in the Czech Republic. It is up to the individual firm to nominate suitable candidates, and to propose the type of training that they will undergo. If the DTI endorses the choice, it will refund up to half of the approved costs.

● Financial aid is also available to companies wishing to become part of a trade mission organised and sponsored by a trade association or other body.

● The World Aid Section holds a large amount of information on projects funded by multilateral development agencies, and maintains a database storing profiles on all related projects, sector reports, tender notices etc.

The European Bank for Reconstruction and Development (EBRD)

The EBRD seeks to encourage the development of a healthy private sector in the Czech Republic, and as a result it has in the past not only offered support to Czech firms, but also funded the restructuring and modernisation of large enterprises and supported SMEs and joint ventures with foreign partners. It also seeks to build up a healthy financial system and extend sources of finance. It normally provides up to 35 per cent of the total cost of a given project through loans, equity and guarantees, and underwriting financing, all at commercial rates of interest. EBRD projects also create demand for suppliers and consultants, and contracts open to British firms are advertised in its *Procurement Opportunities* monthly newsletter.

The Bank will consider most projects, but the Czech Republic is particularly involved in the finance and banking sectors, the energy and telecommunications industries, and in funding environmental schemes. Currently on its books are:

● three public projects, in Czech Telecommunications, Czech Airways and Czech Railways;

● eight regional projects, concentrating on SME support, finance and telecommunications;

● eighteen technical cooperation programmes aimed at project preparation and support in motorways, telecommunications, banking, energy, chemicals, manufacturing, agriculture, wholesale markets, institutional and regional development, business planning, energy efficiency and the environment.

These priorities are not set to change radically – EBRD projects in the near future will concentrate on banking and finance, energy saving and textiles.

The European Investment Bank (EIB)

The European Investment Bank's participation in the EU's development and cooperation policy allows it to offer aid to firms operating in Central and East European countries such as the Czech Republic. It works on a non-profit basis and, in addition to know-how and experience, offers loans at a preferential rate. These loans are tied to specific projects, which are appraised in terms of technical and financial viability and economic and environmental impact. They largely take the form of joint funding, with the EIB offering up to 50 per cent of project costs and working in conjunction with other bodies such as the EBRD and the World Bank. Small- and medium-sized enterprises require third-party bank guarantees.

The EIB's priority sectors include transport and telecommunications, the restructuring and modernisation of the energy sector, and joint ventures and direct investments by EU firms in industry. Recent loans to the Czech Republic have financed small and medium scale manufacturing and tourism projects, modernisation of the transport and telecommunications networks, and upgrading of lignite-fired power stations.

The International Finance Corporation (IFC)

The International Finance Corporation seeks to encourage private sector activity and the development of market economies. The unequalled success of the Czech Republic's privatisation process has meant a rapid expansion of the private sector, in turn bringing continued growth in IFC activities.

The IFC's priorities in the area include:

● aiding the establishment of joint ventures with foreign partners;

● assisting in privatisation and other reforms;

● helping to modernise privatised enterprises and make them efficient and internationally competitive;

● helping to transform the financial sector and build sound capital market institutions;

● assisting small- and medium-sized firms by creating suitable financial intermediaries.

The IFC works in three main ways:

i Financing private sector activity through a number of financial products and services, including loans of between $1m and $100m, equity investments of up to 35 per cent of a company's share capital, and lines of credit etc for SMEs through intermediary institutions (local commercial banks etc). Financing is subject to a number of conditions – notably, projects must be profitable for investors, benefit the economy of the host country, and comply with stringent environmental guidelines. Also, in order to avoid crowding out private companies, the IFC now operates under a new 'non-displacement principle' , by which it will not finance projects which will compete with capital and skills that are already adequately provided by the market. Unlike, for example, the EIB, the IFC charges market rates.

Finance is available to all types of industry, although activities concentrate on infrastructure and financial sector projects. As of the beginning of 1996, financing had been approved in the Czech Republic for projects including support for two building product manufacturers, a beer producer and a privatised bank, and technical assistance to a textile manufacturer planning to modernise and a metal complex seeking to reduce environmental damage.

ii Helping companies to mobilise financing in the international financial markets. The IFC acts primarily as a catalyst, providing a maximum of 25 per cent of financing for any single project, but using its reputation as an endorsement, to increase investor confidence and encourage private sector investment.

iii Providing advice and technical assistance on financial packages, corporate restructuring, privatisation, formulation of business plans and identification of markets, products, technologies, and financial and technical partners. Much of this is carried out through the IFC's Technical Assistance Trust fund.

Businesses setting up in the Czech Republic or expanding their operations there and seeking help can contact the IFC directly – after a preliminary meeting, the IFC will request a detailed feasibility study or business plan. If financing is forthcoming, the Corporation will continue to closely supervise its investment, requiring, for example, quarterly progress reports.

The Know How Fund (KHF)

The Know How Fund aims to facilitate the spread of democracy and free enterprise by backing the transfer of British expertise. Aid to the Czech Republic has in the past focused on banking and finance (about half o the KHF's Czech funds have been spent on the financial sector), public administration and local government, management training and SME development. The Fund's budget for the Czech Republic is now tapering off, as it is one of the most advanced of the Eastern European states, and is simply in less need of assistance. Today, most of the Fund's activities focus on small programmes with grass roots participation, and on the encouragement of study visits by Czechs to Britain to inform them of the options and challenges which they face.

The KHF is still active, however, and will in the future continue to target aid at the areas outlined above, whilst also offering the Czech Republic help in its drive towards EU membership. Future projects include:

● a number of schemes in the banking and the financial sector, funding courses on English for Banking and credit analysis, advice on personnel policy, supervision in banking and insurance, and traning in areas related to EU membership such as foreign trade and anti-dumping;

● help in the adjustment of public administration at all levels to the needs of a market economy, with training programmes for public servants and a Strategic Planning for Prague initiative;

● the Training of Management Trainers Project, aiming to develop management training capacity in the Czech Republic;

● the reduction of regional pockets of high unemployment by offering advice in areas such as youth training, and the provision of help for business agencies and SME development.

A number of projects are open to British firms, who should register details of their interests and expertise with the Contracts Branch of the Overseas Development Association in order to be considered when future contracts are put out to tender. The KHF also welcomes proposals for projects, providing that they fall within its priority sectors, and encourage the process of economic or political transition – applicants should contact the Fund before preparing a detailed proposal. In projects funded entirely by the KHF, competitive tendering is the norm, and disbursements are usually tied to British companies.

KHF Investment Schemes

The KHF runs two programmes of interest to those seeking to invest in the Czech Republic (although the defence equipment and tobacco sectors are excluded). The Pre-Investment Feasibility Studies scheme (PIFS) is available to those firms which have already undertaken basic market research and are considering long-term investment in the Czech Republic, and can provide up to 50 per cent of the cost of research into the commercial and financial viability of the project. The Training for Investment Personnel Scheme (TIPS) offers aid to those training Czech investment operations personnel in management and business skills. Tel: 0171 210 0048 for further information.

The Phare Programme

The Phare Programme is administered by the EU, and provides grant financing for economic and development projects aimed at the creation of market economies open to untrammelled private enterprise. Aid takes the form of investment support (studies, capital grants, guarantees and credit lines), infrastructural investment and know-how (policy advice, technical expertise, training, consultancy work, the development of legislation and institutions etc.)

Phare activities in the Czech Republic now focus on preparing the Czech Republic for entry into the European Union. Targeted areas for the period 1995–1999 include the following:

● Legislative integration, with technical support, training and equipment supply to encourage the reform of competition law, social protection provision etc.

● Institutional integration, focusing on the reform of public administration to ensure that Czech public services correspond with EU standards, and that public institutions vital to the market economy (eg customs, standards etc) are in place.

● Infrastructural integration, with the provision of funds for high priority improvements in trans-European and cross-border communications links.

● Social and economic development in areas where there is a role for public support, eg SME, export and regional development, the agricultural and energy sectors, employment services, social insurance and management training.

● The promotion of foreign investment through the CzechInvest agency.

A technical assistance fund also makes quantities of funding available for projects supported by the government but not covered by individual sector programmes.

Aid is also available in the form of a number of multi-country programmes – notably the programmes for cross-border cooperation, active in Western and Northern Bohemia (areas adjacent to Germany and Austria). Six projects are now in an advanced stage of preparation, with funds allotted to:

● the transport sector, for the improvement of the Decin-Prague-Breclav railway line and a number of E-roads;

● the energy sector, aimed at reducing energy consumption and pollution and modernising supply systems;

● the rehabilitation of historical monuments;

● the construction and modernisation of systems for sewage disposal and treatment, waste management and treatment of toxic soils;

● the removal of barriers to economic development in the area, and the creation of a sound infrastructure and healthy private sector;

● the diversification of agricultural incomes and the promotion of cross-border cooperation in rural development and marketing;

● cross-border cooperation in employment schemes and vocational training.

Allocation of Phare funds is decided at a national level, jointly by the EC and the Czech government. Specific projects are administered on the ground by Project Management Units (PMUs) in the various sectors, which also deal with tenders and contracts for supplies and services. UK companies can initiate projects, but should contact the relevant organisations and PMUs in the Czech Republic. Working in this way may reduce the possibility of the project going out to competitive tender. Registration on the Phare Central Consultancy Register (CCR) is advised, although not compulsory, for any firms that wish to provide services or supplies within the programme.

For more information contact the Phare Information Office or alternatively the DTI's World Aid Section, whose database contains details of projects and programmes already funded under Phare.

The Joint Venture Phare Programme (JOPP)

A part of the main EC programme, JOPP aims to hasten the development of the Czech SME sector by encouraging external investment by those SMEs in EU countries wishing to launch joint ventures with Czech firms.

JOPP offers support to joint ventures at various stages of their development:

● At the preliminary stage, the programme can help fund market analysis, business plans, contract negotiations, production of prototypes, pilot projects and pre-feasibility studies.

● At the co-financing stage, JOPP provides medium- to long-term finance for joint ventures, on condition that other investors make similar commitments.

● At the technical assistance phase, the programme provides up to 50 per cent of the eligible costs of transferring know-how to the workforce up to a maximum of ECU 150,000.

The United Nations

While the UK does not offer aid per se to those wishing to do business in the Czech Republic, its various agencies have extensive procurement needs in the country, and tenders are often open to British firms. The most important source of contracts is the United Nations Industrial Development Organisation (UNIDO), which carries out industrial studies and encourages the transfer of technology and know how. Prospective contractors should complete the 'UNIDO Roster of Consulting Organisations' while equipment suppliers should complete the 'Questionnaire for UNIDO Roster of Vendors'. There is a UK Investment Promotion coordinator at UNIDO dedicated to identifying opportunities for British companies:

Industrial Investment Division
UNIDO
Vienna International Centre
PO Box 300
A-1400 Vienna
Tel: +1 431 211 31 3084
Fax: +1 431 230 8260
Contact: Stuart Heaman-Dunn

The World Bank

At the moment the World Bank have no ongoing projects in the Czech Republic, whose government has (due to the rapid development of the country) expressed no wish to receive loans, although the Bank is more than willing to offer its help

Appendix II

Further Sources of Information

Department of Trade and Industry

Department of Trade and Industry
Bay 748, Kingsgate House
66–74 Victoria Street
London SW1E 6SW
United Kingdom
Tel: +44 171 215 8446
Fax: +44 171 215 4743
Contact: Kevin Ringham, Desk Officer - Czech and Slovak Republics
OR
Tel/Fax: +44 1525 220 529
John Woodcock, Export Promoter for the Czech and Slovak Republics

Responsible for UK trade promotion and for giving advice and providing information on the market for companies wishing to export to, and invest in, the Czech Republic.

East European Trade Council
10 Westminster Palace Gardens
Artillery Row
London SW1P 1RL
United Kingdom
Tel: +44 171 222 7622
Fax: +44 171 222 5359
Contact: James McNeish, Director

Area advisory group of the DTI. Maintains a library dedicated to business publications concerning eastern Europe and the FSU.

Export Market Information Centre (EMIC)
Room 134
66–74 Victoria Street
London SW1E 6SW
United Kingdom
Tel: +44 171 215 5444/5445

The Export Market Information Centre is provided by the DTI to enable the business person to research overseas export markets. Information available includes statistics, directories, market research reports, mail order catalogues and country reports.

Embassies

British Embassy
Thunovska 14
118 00 Prague 1
Czech Republic
Tel: +42 2 2451 0439/0443
Fax: +42 2 2451 1314

British Embassy
Commercial Section
Jungmanova 30
110 00 Prague 1
Czech Republic
Tel: +42 2 2421 2876/2909
Fax: +42 2 2423 0997
Contact: Mike Connor, First Secretary (commercial)

Provides advice and assistance in the market, working closely in conjuction with the DTI through the Overseas Trade Services.

Economic and Commercial Section
Embassy of the Czech Republic
26 Kensington Palace Gardens
London W8 4QY
United Kingdom
Tel: +44 171 243 1115
Fax: +44 171 727 9654
Contact: Karel Andropius, Commercial Counsellor

The Economic and Commercial Section deals with exports from the Czech Republic, including those to the United Kingdom, and can also give assistance to those seeking to set up offices in the Czech Republic.

Embassy of the USA
Trziste 15
118 01 Prague 1
Czech Republic
Tel: +42 2 2451 0847
Fax: +42 2 2451 1001
Contact: Mr Douglas Hengel, Political and Economic counsellor

German Embassy
Vlasska 19
11801 Prague 1
Czech Republic
Tel: +42 2 2451 0323
Fax: +42 2 2451 0156
Contact: Joachim Hacker, Economic Counsellor

British Business Organisations

British Czech and Slovak Association
522 Finchley Road
London NW11 8DD
United Kingdom
Tel: +44 181 458 1777
Contact: Maria Hughes, Business Circle Coordinator

British Invisibles
Windsor House
39 King Street
London EC2 8DQ
United Kingdom
Tel: +44 171 600 1198
Fax: +44 171 606 4248
Contact: Neil Jaggers, Director, Eastern Europe

City Network for East-West Trade (CeeNet)
Warnford Court
Throgmorton Street
London EC2N 2AT
United Kingdom
Tel: +44 171 638 9299
Fax: +44 171 588 8555

Confederation of British Industry
Centre Point
103 New Oxford Street
London WC1A 1DU
United Kingdom
Tel: +44 171 379 7400
Fax: +44 171 240 2651
Contact: Pauline Shearman

Financial Aid

The British Council

General advice:

British Council
Export Promotion Unit
10 Spring Gardens
London SW1A 2BN
United Kingdom
Tel: +44 171 389 4836
Fax: +44 171 389 4589
Contact: Peter Mackenzie Smith
                            ﹍d ma﹍

British Council
Central Management of Direct Teaching
10 Spring Gardens
London SW1A 2BN
United Kingdom
Tel: +44 171 389 4374
Fax: +44 171 389 4140
Contact: Mike Thornton, Projects and
Marketing Officer

British Council
Development and Training Services
Medlock Street
Manchester
United Kingdom
Tel: +44 161 957 7843
Fax: +44 161 957 7831
Contact: Jim Taylor, David Knox,
Europe Group

Management of sponsored events:

British Council
Head of Business Relations Unit
10 Spring Gardens
London SW1A 2BN

United Kingdom
Tel: +44 171 389 4940
Fax: +44 171 389 4971
Contact: David Blagborough

Office in the Czech Republic:

British Council
Narodni 10
125 01 Prague 1
Czech Republic
Tel: +42 2 2491 2179/83
Fax: +42 2 2491 3839
Contact: Mary O'Neill, Director

The European Bank for Reconstruction and Development

EBRD
One Exchange Square
London EC2A 2EH
United Kingdom
Tel: +44 171 338 6000
Fax: +44 171 338 6100
http.//www.ebird.com
Contact: Jiri Huebner

EBRD - Resident Office
Korlova 27
1101 Prague 1
Czech Republic
Tel: +42 2 2423 9070
Fax: +42 2 2423 3077
Contact: Igor Ocka, Senior Banker

The European Investment Bank

European Investment Bank
London Office
68 Pall Mall
London SW1Y 5ES
United Kingdom
Tel: +44 171 343 1200
Fax: +44 171 930 9929

European Investment Bank
100 Boulevard Konrad Adenauer
L–2950 Luxembourg
Tel: +35 2 4379 4304
Fax: +35 2 4379 4350

International Finance Corporation

The International Finance
Corporation
European Office
4 Millbank
London SW1P 3JA
United Kingdom
Tel: +44 171 222 7711
Fax: +44 171 976 8323

The Know How Fund

General enquiries:
The Know How Fund
Room J1–14
Old Admiralty Building
Whitehall
London SW1A 2AF
United Kingdom
Tel: +44 171 210 0006
Fax: +44 171 210 0010
Contact: Chris Smart

Contracts Branch:
Overseas Development
Administration
Abercrombie House
Eaglesham Road
East Kilbride
Glasgow G75 8EA
Scotland
United Kingdom
Tel: +44 135 584 4000
Fax: +44 135 584 3499

The Know How Fund runs a
number of schemes of interest to firms

setting up in the Czech Republic,
including Pre-Investment Feasibility
Studies (PIFS), which can provide up
to 50 per cent of the cost of a pre-
investment study, and the Training
for Investment Personnel Scheme
(TIPS), which helps fund the training
of indigenous personnel:

Investment Schemes Section
Know How Fund
Foreign and Commonwealth Office
Old Admiralty Building
Whitehall
London SW1A 2AF
United Kingdom
Tel: +44 171 210 0023
Fax: +44 171 210 0010
Contact: Peter Goold

Phare

Central Consultancy Register
Rue Saint Georges
Sint Jorisstraat 32
B–1050 Brussels
Belgium
Tel: +32 2 644 0951/3713
Fax: +32 2 644 1599
Contact: Sylvie Davrou-Koch,
Programme Manager

JOPP Assistance Unit
Batiment Wagner
Rue Alcide de Gasperi
2920 Luxembourg
Tel: +352 467 096
Fax: +352 467 097

National Co-ordinator of the Phare
programme in the Czech Republic c/o
Centre for Foreign Assistance (CFA)
Ministry of Economy of the Czech
Republic
Staromestske Namesti 6

110 15 Prague 1
Tel: +42 2 2486 1349
Fax: +42 2 231 3227/232 6062

Phare Information Office
DG1A
Commission of the European
Communities
Rue d'Arlon 88
1040 Brussels
Belgium
Tel: +32 2 2991 400/600
Fax: +32 2 2991 777

World Aid Section
Department of Trade and Industry
Kingsgate House
66–74 Victoria Street
London SW1E 6SW
Tel: +44 171 215 4654
Fax: +44 171 913 0397

Phare Programme Management Units
(PMUs):

Agriculture Programme
Ministry of Agriculture
Tesnov 17
110 00 Prague 1
Czech Republic
Tel: +42 2 218 12 385
Fax: +42 2 248 10 652
Contact: Ludek Broz

Banking Programme
Czech National Bank
Na Prikope 28
110 03 Prague 1
Czech Republic
Tel: +42 2 244 12 022/14 459
Fax: +42 2 244 12 574
*Contact: Premysl Micka, Jan Malek,
Directors*

Cross-border cooperation programme
(CBC)
Ministry of Economy
Phare cross-border cooperation
Letenska 3
110 00 Prague 1
Czech Republic
Tel: +42 2 245 11 479
Fax: +42 2 53 79 47/53 79 44
Contact: Richard Mundil, Director

Customs Administration Programme
General Directorate of Customs
Washingtonova 11
113 54 Prague 1
Czech Republic
Tel: +42 2 242 28 742
Fax: +42 2 240 63 040
*Contacts: Vendulka Hola, Lubomir
Moravcik*

Energy Programme
EU Energy Centre 'THERMIE'
Praha
Soukenicka 23
110 00 Prague 1
Czech Republic
Tel: +42 2 231 56 15
Fax: +42 2 231 56 35
Contact: Antonin Martinek

Enterprise Restructuring and
Privatisation Programme
PMU EXDEV - Room 802
Vrsovicka 65
101 60 Prague 10
Czech Republic
Tel: +42 2 671 22 026/948/810/468/982
Fax: +42 2 671 32 517
Contact: Lubomir Civin, Director

Environment Programme
Ministry of the Environment
Vrsovicka 65
101 60 Prague 10

Czech Republic
Tel: +42 2 671 22 218/369
Fax: +42 2 673 10 490
Contact: Alexandra Orlikova, Director

Finance Programme
Ministry of Finance - PMU Phare
Letenska 15
110 00 Prague 1
Czech Republic
Tel: +42 2 245 42 612/43 009
Fax: +42 2 245 11 222
*Contact: Jana Stara, Dagmar
Muhlbachova, Directors*

Nuclear Safety Programme
State Office for Nuclear Safety
Slezska 9
120 29 Prague 2
Czech Republic
Tel: +42 2 241 71 111
Fax: +42 2 241 72 467
*Contact: Dana Prochazkova,
Responsible Officer*

Regional and Local Economic
Development Programme
Letenska 3
110 00 Prague 1
Czech Republic
Tel: +42 2 245 10 898/248 62 220
Fax: +42 2 537 940

North Bohemia:
Regional Economic Development
Unit
Budovatelu 2830/C
434 00 Most
Tel: +42 35 34 65 38/39
Fax: +42 35 43 65 38

North Moravia:
Regional Enterprise Fund
Zerotinova 1
702 00 Ostrava

Tel: +42 69 23 22 73/32 21/50 62
Fax: +42 69 23 22 13

Research and Development
Programme
Czech Technical University
Zikova 4
160 00 Prague 6
Czech Republic
Tel: +42 2 332 12 975/243 10 790
Fax: +42 2 243 10 271
Contact: Jan Gruntorad, Manager

Risk Capital Fund
Konviktska 5
110 00 Prague 1
Czech Republic
Tel: +42 2 242 29 422–28
Fax: +42 2 264 995/242 27 873
Contact: Michael Nosek, Director

Small-and Medium-Sized Enterprises
Programme
Business Development Agency
Letenska 3
118 01 Prague 1
Czech Republic
Tel: +42 2 53 02 56
Fax: +42 2 53 79 49
Contact: Miroslav Hradil, Director

Telecommunications Programme
Czech Telecommunications Office
Klimentska 27
125 02 Prague 1
Czech Republic
Tel: +42 2 24 91 03 46
Fax: +42 2 24 91 25 56
Contact: Nada Paclova, Director

Transport Programme
Finance and Economics Department
Ministry of Transport
Nabrezi L Svobody 12
110 15 Prague 1

Czech Republic
Tel: +42 2 230 31 147
Fax: +42 2 248 12 339
Contact: Ludmila Lefnerova, Director

The World Bank

The World Bank
1818 H Street N.W.
Washington DC
20433
USA
Tel: +1 202 477 1234
Fax: +1 202 477 1034
Contact: Ulrich Hewer

European Union

DG1A/B/3 European Commission
200 Rue de la Loi
1049 Brussels
Belgium
Tel: +3 22 295 8266
Fax: +3 22 295 8094
Contact: Marco Franco

European Commission Delegation in
the Czech Republic
PO Box 292
16041 Prague 6
Czech Republic
Tel: +42 2 325 051
Fax: +42 2 311 0860

Mission of the Czech Republic to the
EU in Brussels
Rue Engelandstraat 555
1180 Brussels
Belgium
Tel: +32 2 375 93 34/43
Fax: +32 2 375 22 46
Contact: Jiri Zukal, First Secretary

Representation of the European
Commission in the UK
8 Storey's Gate
London SW1P 3AT
United Kingdom
Tel: +44 171 973 1992
Fax: +44 171 973 1900/1910

Chambers of Commerce

American Chamber of Commerce
Karlovo namesti 24
110 00 Prague 1
Czech Republic
Tel: +42 2 299 887/296 778
Fax: +42 2 291 481
Contact: Helena Stolka

Birmingham Chamber of Commerce
and Industry
PO Box 360
75 Harborne Road
Birmingham B15 3DH
United Kingdom
Tel: +44 121 454 6171
Fax: +44 121 455 8670
*Contact: Helen Whistance, Export
Market Office*

Czech-German Chamber of Commerce
and Industry
Masarykova nabrezi 30
110 00 Prague 1
Czech Republic
Tel: +42 2 298 051-5
Fax: +42 2 2491 3827
Contact: Dieter Mankowski

Economic Chamber of the Czech
Republic
Argentinska 38
170 05 Prague 7
Czech Republic
Tel: +42 2 875 344

Fax: +42 2 804 894
Contact: Vladimir Prokop

London Chamber of Commerce and
Industry
33 Queen Street
London EC4R 1AP
United Kingdom
Tel: +44 171 248 4444
Fax: +44 171 489 0391
*Contact: Robert Anthony, World Trade
Executive*

Manchester Chamber of Commerce
and Industry
56 Oxford Street
Manchester M60 7HJ
United Kingdom
Tel: +44 161 236 3210
Fax: +44 161 236 4160
*Contact: International Trade
Department*

Czech Official Bodies

**Note: Government Ministries
are currently undergoing
reorganisation - most contact
names and addresses will change.
Some ministries (eg Privatisation)
are to be dissolved. The new
information should be available
by the middle of August.**

Centre for Foreign Economic
Relations
Politickych veznu 20
PO Box 791
111 21 Prague 1
Czech Republic
Tel: +42 2 2422 1586/2406 2421
Fax: +42 2 2422 1575

Czech Board of Mines
Kozi 4
110 01 Prague 1
Czech Republic
Tel: +42 2 2481 2447
Fax: +42 2 269 506

Czech National Bank
Na Prikope 28
110 03 Prague 1
Czech Republic
Tel: +42 2 244 1111
Fax: +42 2 242 17865/18522

Czechoslovak Management Center
nam. 5. kvetna 2
250 88 Celakovice
Czech Republic
Tel: +42 2 2029 1441

Czech Stock Exchange
Rybna 14
110 00 Prague 1
Czech Republic
Tel: +42 2 2180 1111
Fax: +42 2 2180 2191

General Board of Customs
Washingtonova 11
110 00 Prague 1
Czech Republic
Tel: +42 2 2406 1111
Fax: +42 2 2406 2639/3040

Union of Professional Unions
Skretova 6
120 59 Prague 2
Czech Republic
Tel: +42 2 2423 0561
Fax: +42 2 2423 0570

CzechInvest

Czechinvest
95 Great Portland Street
London W1N 5RA
United Kingom
Tel: +44 171 291 9922
Fax: +44 171 436 8300
Contact: Lubor Veleba

CzechInvest
Politickych veznu 20
112 49 Prague 1
Czech Republic
Tel: +42 2 2422 1540
Fax: +42 2 2422 1804

Regional Representatives

Brno:
Magistrat mesta Brno
Zelny trh 13
601 67 Brno
Tel and fax: +42 5 4221 2095
Contact: Radek Vetecnik

Hradec Kralove:
Magistrat mesta Hradec Kralove
Ulrichovo nam. 1
520 10 Hradec Kralove
Tel: +42 49 5751 450
Fax: +42 49 255 79
Contact: Zdenek Hofman

Most:
Regionalni rozvojova agentura, a.s.
Budovatelu 2830
434 01 Most
Tel: +42 35 346 538-9
Fax: +42 35 249 80
Contact: Manfred Hellmich

Novy Jicin:
Mestsky urad Novy Jicin
Masarykovo nam. 1

741 11 Novy Jicin
Tel: +42 656 702 280/701 052
Fax: +42 656 701 188
Contact: Karel Kozelsky

Olomouc:
Okresni urad Olomouc
Krizkovskeho 6
772 00 Olomouc
Tel: +42 68 5222 944
Fax: +42 68 5223 183
Contact: Frantisek Kastyl

Ostrava:
Agentura pro regionalni rozvoj
Podebradova 16
702 00 Ostrava
Tel: +42 69 234 677
Fax: +42 69 234 695
Contact: Petr Czekaj

Pardubice:
Magistrat mesta Pardubic
Pernstynske nam. 1
530 21 Pardubice
Tel: +42 40 6859 504/516
Fax: +42 40 514 083
Contact: Gabriela Svobodova

Plzen:
Magistrat mesta Plzne
Utvar koncepce a rozvoje
Skroupova 5
305 84 Plzen
Tel: +42 19 7163 400/7221 402
Fax: +42 19 7221 402
Contact: Jaroslav Pojar

Zlin:
Urad mesta Zlina
trida T. Bati 44
761 40 Zlin
Tel and fax: +42 67 529 142
Contact: Petr Hunak

Znojmo:
Mestsky urad Znojmo
Znojemsky rozvojovy fond
Obrokova 10
669 01 Znojmo
Tel: +42 624 225 528
Fax: +42 624 224 229
Contact: Ladislav Skopal

Czech Professional Associations

Association for Business Consultancy
Slezska 7
120 56 Prague 2
Czech Republic
Tel: +42 2 256 276
Fax: +42 2 258 550

Association for the Quality Prize of
the Czech Republic
Novotneho lavka 5
116 68 Prague 1
Czech Republic
Tel: +42 2 2108 2301
Fax: +42 2 2108 2238
Contact: Vladimir Straka

Association of Czech Entrepreneurs
Skretova 6/44
120 59 Prague 2
Czech Republic
Tel and Fax: +42 2 2423 0572
Contact: Vaclav Smolak

Association of Investment Companies
and Funds
Spalena 51
110 00 Prague 1
Czech Republic
Tel: +42 2 296 108
Fax: +42 2 291 710
Contact: Jan Suchanek

Association of Real Property Bureaus
Jugoslavska 23
120 00 Prague 2
Czech Republic
Tel: +42 2 253 829/259 594
Fax: +42 2 259 594
Contact: Pavel Dvorsky

Association of Securities Dealers and
Brokers
Na Pankraci 11
140 00 Prague 4
Czech Republic
Tel: +42 2 421 829
Fax: +42 2 422 181
*Contacts: Jiri Vavra, Ladislav
Novotny*

Banking Association
Vodickova ulice 30
110 00 Prague 1
Czech Republic
Tel: +42 2 2422 5926
Fax: +42 2 2422 5957
Contact: Ivan Angelis

Chamber of Commercial Lawyers
Senovazne nam. 23
110 00 Prague 1
Czech Republic
Tel: +42 2 2414 2457-9
Fax: +42 2 2414 2415
Contact: Lygie Snaselova

Chamber of Tax Advisors
PO Box 121
657 21 Brno 2
Tel: +42 5 42321 306/282
Fax: +42 5 4221 0328

Confederation of Industry of the
Czech Republic
Mikulandska 7
113 61 Prague 1
Czech Republic

Tel: +42 2 2491 5679
Fax: +42 2 297 896
e-mail: spcr@spcr.ant.cz
Contact: Otto Emanovsky

Czech Association of Managers
Podolska 50
147 00 Prague 4
Czech Republic
Tel: +42 2 6121 4111
Contact: Jiri Styblo

Czech Chamber of Lawyers
Narodni 16
110 00 Prague 1
Czech Republic
Tel: +42 2 2491 3606
Fax: +42 2 2491 0162
Contact: Vaclav Mandak

Czech Quality Association
Novotneho lavka 5
116 68 Prague 1
Czech Republic
Tel: +42 2 2108 2345
Fax: +42 2 2108 2229
Contact: Vladimir Votapek

Czech Free Zones and Free Warehouses

Cheb:
Senzo Cheb
Svobody 25
350 01 Cheb

Hradec Kralove:
Merka Spedition
Warehouse Area 857
500 03 Hradec Kralove

Ostrava:
Free Zone Ostrava
Gorkeho 8
728 88 Ostrava 1

Pardubice:
Free Zone Pardubice
Pernstynske nam. 1
530 21 Pardubice

Prague:
CSAD Praha
Hybernska 32
111 21 Prague 1

Cs Management Praha
(operator of the Dutyfree Zone
Vysocany-Bor u Tachova)
K sancim 50
163 00 Prague 6

Exces
Tiskarska 563/6
100 00 Prague 10

SPEDQUIC
Free Warehouse in Frantiskov nad
Ploucnici
Lukasova 7
130 00 Prague 3

Trinec:
Trinecke zelezarny
739 70 Trinec

Zlin:
Graddo Zlin
PO 231
760 01 Zlin

Timexis
Free zone Uherske Hradiste-Kunovice
Moravska 4779
660 05 Zlin

Sources of Information

Adam Smith Institute
11/13 Charter House Buildings
London EClM 7AN
United Kingdom
Tel: +44 171490 3774
Fax: +44 171490 8932

Aspect
Mikulandska 10
110 00 Prague 1
Czech Republic
Tel: +42 2 24914333
Fax: +42 2 24915677

Business Central Europe
Economist
PO Box 14
Harolds Hill
Romford
Essex RM3 8EQ
United Kingdom
Tel: +44 1708 381555
Fax: +44 1708 381211
Czech Business and Trade
PP Agency
V Jircharich 150/8
110 00 Prague 1
Czech Republic
Tel: +42 2 24912185
Fax: +42 2 24912355

Czech Information Centre
Economic Section
95 Great Portland Street
London W1N 5RA
United Kingdom
 Tel: +44 171 436 3200
Fax: +44 171 436 8300
Contact: Michael Mares, Director

Czech Statistical Office
Sokolovska 142
180 00 Prague 8

Czech Republic
Tel: +42 2 6604 1111
Fax: +42 2 6631 1243

Dun and Bradstreet
Holmes Farm Way
High Wycombe
Buckinghamshire HP12 4UL
United Kingdom
Tel: +44 1494 423689
Fax: +44 1494 422332

Euroforum
14 Bowden Street
London SE11 4DS
United Kingdom
Tel: +44 171878 6886
Fax: +44 171878 6887

Euro Info Centre North West
Liverpool Central Libraries William
Brown
Liverpool L3 8EW
United Kingdom
Tel: +44 151 298 1928
Fax: +44 151 207 1342
*Contact: Val Anderton, Business
Development Officer*

EURO INFO CENTRUM
Havelkova 22
130 00 Prague 3
Tel: +42 2 2423 1486 and 2100
8334/8277/8462
Fax: +42 2 2423 1114

European Information Network
Plzenska 181
150 00 Prague 5
Czech Republic
Tel: +42 2 524 474
Internet: http://www.ceo.lz/
*Contacts: David Rothstein, Gina
Fratto*

Financial Times
Maple House
149 Tottenham Court Road
London WIP 9LL
United Kingdom
Tel: +44 171 896 2222
Fax: +44 171896 2274

Golden Pages (Zlate Stranky)
Meditel
Na Florenci 29
110 00 Prague 1
Czech Republic
Tel: +42 2 236 7479
Fax: +42 2 232 6988

Inform Katalog
c/o VP International
Redhill House
Chester CH4 8BU
United Kingdom
Tel: +44 1244 681 619
Fax: +44 1244 681617

Kompass
Reed Information Services
Windsor Court
East Grinstead House
East Grinstead
West Sussex R819 lXA
United Kingdom
Tel: +44 1342 326972
Fax: +44 1342 335612

MAX Business Advisor
Taboritska 23
130 87 Prague 3
Czech Republic
Tel: +42 2 6709 2457
Fax: +42 2 273406

NIS (National Information Centre of
the Czech Republic)
Havelkova 22
130 00 Prague 3

Czech Republic
Tel: +42 2 2421 5808-15/2422 2026-9
Fax: +42 2 2422 1484/3177

PIS (Prague Information Service)
Za Poricskou branou 7
180 00 Prague 8
Czech Republic
Tel: +42 2 2481 6153
Fax: +42 2 2311 124

Tradelinks
c/o VP International
Redhill House
Chester CH4 8BU
United Kingdom
Tel: +44 1244 681619
Fax: +44 1244 681 617

United Nations Information Centre
Panska 5
110 00 Prague 1
Czech Republic
Tel /Fax: +42 2 2423 0574

Vystavista Prague
c/o VP International
Redhill House
Chester CH4 8BU
United Kingdom
Tel: +44 1244 681 619
Fax: +44 1244 681 617

Czech Banks in London

Ceskoslovenska Obchodni Banka
London Representative Office
20 St Dunstan's Hill
London EC3R 8HL
United Kingdom
Tel: +44 171 338 0804
Fax: +44 171 338 0805

Komercni Banka
London Representative Office
35 Moorgate
London EC2R 6BT
United Kingdom
Tel: +44 171 588 7125
Fax: +44 171 588 7120

Zivnostenska Banka
Phoenix House
18 King William Street
London EC4N 7BY
United Kingdom
Tel: +44 171 283 3333
Fax: +44 171 621 0093

Brno Fair

The long-established Brno fair is one
of the main ways of doing business in
the Czech Republic

British Agents for the Brno Fair:

John Haigh Services
Attwell House
1-3 Attwell Road
Peckham
London SE15 4TW
United Kingdom
Tel: +44 171 639 7265
Fax: +44 171 358 0966
Contact: John Haigh

BVV
Vystaviste 1
PO Box 491
660 91 Brno
Tel: +42 5 314 1111
Fax: +42 5 325 640

Appendix III

Contact Addresses

Anglo-Czechoslovak Ventures Ltd
44 Swain's Lane
London N6 6QR
United Kingdom
Tel: +44 171 284 0091
Fax: +44 171 267 8392
Contact: Micheal Hermann

**AWS Corporate Finance &
Consultancy**
Copperfields
Harlequin Lane
Crowborough
East Sussex TN6 1HU
United Kingdom
Tel/Fax: +44 1892 667 891

**AWS Corporate Finance &
Consultancy**
Aspen House
67 Wimbledon Road
Bridgewater
Somerset
TA6 7DR
Tel: +44 1278 445151
Fax: +44 1278 445152

Cerrex Ltd
6th Floor
National House
60–66 Wardour Street
London W1V 3HP
United Kingdom
Tel: +44 171 734 2879
Fax: +44 1923 858013
Contact: Michael Bird,
Martin A Doherty

Česká Pojišt'ovna
Spalena 16
113 04 Prague 1
Czech Republic
Tel: +422 2424 1058
Fax: +422 2424 1067
Contact: Josef Čižek

Creditanstalt
Schottengasse 6
A–1010 Vienna
Austria
Tel: +431 531 310
Fax: +431 531 311644
Contact: Christian Kaltenegger

CzechInvest
Politických veznu 20
112 49 Prague 1
Czech Republic
Tel: +42 2 2422 1540
Fax: +42 2 2422 1804/2406 2208
Contact: Aleš Ždimera

CEE Telecoms Projects
Central and Eastern European
Telecommunication
Marketing Service
61 Stanhope Avenue
London N3 3LY
United Kingdom
Tel: +44 181 346 6852
Fax: +44 181 349 2452
e-mail: isloboda@ieeorg
Contact: Ivan Sloboda

GJW Government Relations
Rue des Patriotes 28
B–1000 Brussels
Belgium
Tel: +32 2 735 9494
Fax: +32 2 734 2715
Contact: Andrew Ellis

GJW Prague
Revoluční 3
110 15 Prague 1
Czech Republic
Tel: +42 2 481 5119
Fax: +42 2 481 0261
Contact: Vladimir Feldman

Gleeds
Konviktska 24
110 00 Prague 1
Czech Republic
Tel: +42 2 24 23 18 83
Fax: +42 2 24 23 19 20
Contact: David Lawn

HSBC Investment Services sro
Narodni 10
110 00 Praha 1
Czech Republic
Tel: +42 2 2495 1510
Fax: +42 2 2491 2370
Contact: Jan Tauber

Lubbock Fine sro
Narodni trida 9
110 00 Prague 1
Czech Republic
Tel: +422 2481 1415
Fax: +422 232 4706
e-mail: 100070.2307@compuserve.com
Contact: Martin Levey

McKenna & Co
Mitre House
160 Aldersgate Street
London EC1A 4DD
United Kingdom
Tel: +44 171 606 9000
Fax: +44 171 606 9100
e-mail: infodesk@mckenna.co.uk
Contact: Irena Edwards

PA Consulting Group
Thámova 9
186 00 Prague 8
Czech Republic
Tel: +42 2 2481 1869
Fax: +42 2 232 96 64
Contact: John Waugh

Prokop International Ltd
7 Chelsea Embankment
London SW3 4LF
United Kingdom
Tel: +44 171 352 2724
Fax: +44 171 351 5284
Contact: Michael Prokop

Research International World Service
6/7 Grosvenor Place
London SW1X 7SH
United Kingdom
Tel: +44 171 656 5000
Fax: +44 171 235 4170
Contact: Mia Bartonova

Seddons Solicitors
5 Portman Square
London W1H 0NT
United Kingdom
Tel: +44 171 486 9681
Fax: +44 171 935 5049
e-mail: postmaster@seddons.co.uk
Contact: Jan Grozdanovic

Seddons Solicitors
Rybna 1
110 00 Prague 1
Czech Reppublic
Tel: +42 2 231 6522/6532
Fax: +42 2 231 6805
e-mail: seddons@terminal.cz
Contact: Karin Pomaizlova

VP International
Red Hill House
Hope Street
Chester CH4 8BU
United Kingdom
Tel: +44 1244 681619
Fax: +44 1244 681617
Contact: Nick Sljivic

Appendix IV

Recommended Reading

Journals

British Czech and Slovak Association Newsletter, bi-monthly, London

Business Europa: Central Business Magazine, Walden Publishing Group, Essex

Central European Business Weekly, VP International, Chester

Czech Republic Country Report, quarterly and Country Profile, yearly, Economist Intelligence Unit, London

Prague Business Journal, VP International, Chester

New Markets Monthly, monthly, BSB Publishing, Dorking

Books

Albertina Company Register, CD-ROM

Business Law Guide to the Czech Republic, CCH Editions, 1994

Businessman's Guide to Legislation in 1995-6, VP International, Chester 1995

Doing Business with the Czech Republic, DTI and FCO, London 1995

Doing Business in the Czech Republic, Ernst & Young, New York 1994

Doing Business in the Czech Republic, PP Agency, Prague 1996

Doing Business in the Czech and Slovak Republics, Price Waterhouse, London 1993

Industry in the Czech and Slovak Republics, OECD, Stationary Office Agencies, London 1994

Investing, Licensing and Trading Conditions Abroad - Czech Republic, Economist Intelligence Unit, London 1994

Kompass: Czech Republic (business information directory), Reed Information Services

Privatisation in the Czech and Slovak Republics, VP International, Chester 1993

Real Estate in the Czech and Slovak Republics, VP International, Chester 1994

Resources (reference guide with quarterly updates)
(Resources, PO Box 352, 110 00 Prague 1)

Selected Economic and Social Development Indicators, Czech Statistical Office, Prague 1994

The Prague Post 1996 Book of Lists, Prague 1996

Index

Index of Advertisers